Outdoor Cooking

GENERAL EDITOR
CHUCK WILLIAMS

RECIPES
JOHN PHILLIP CARROLL

PHOTOGRAPHY
ALLAN ROSENBERG

TIME
LIFE
BOOKS

TIME-LIFE BOOKS
Time-Life Books is a division of Time Life Inc.
Time-Life is a trademark of Time Warner Inc. U.S.A.

Time-Life Custom Publishing
Vice President and Publisher: Terry Newell
Managing Editor: Donia Ann Steele
Director of New Product Development: Quentin McAndrew
Vice President of Sales and Marketing: Neil Levin
Director of Financial Operations: J. Brian Birky

WILLIAMS-SONOMA
Founder/Vice-Chairman: Chuck Williams
Book Buyer: Victoria Kalish

WELDON OWEN INC.
President: John Owen
Vice President and Publisher: Wendely Harvey
CFO: Larry Partington
Managing Editor: Lisa Chaney Atwood
Editor: Hannah Rahill
Consulting Editor: Norman Kolpas
Copy Editor: Sharon Silva
Design: John Bull, The Book Design Company
Production Director: Stephanie Sherman
Production Coordinator: Tarji Mickelson
Editorial Assistant: Sarah Lemas
Vice President International Sales: Stuart Laurence
Co-Editions Director: Derek Barton
Food Photographer: Allan Rosenberg
Additional Food Photography: Allen V. Lott
Primary Food Stylist: Heidi Gintner
Prop Stylist: Sandra Griswold
Assistant Food Stylist: Elizabeth C. Davis
Glossary Illustrations: Alice Harth

The Williams-Sonoma Kitchen Library
conceived and produced by Weldon Owen Inc.
814 Montgomery St., San Francisco, CA 94133

In collaboration with Williams-Sonoma
3250 Van Ness Ave., San Francisco, CA 94109

Printed in China

A Note on Weights and Measures:
All recipes include customary U.S. and metric measurements. Metric conversions are based on a standard developed for these books and have been rounded off. Actual weights may vary.

A Weldon Owen Production

Copyright © 1997 Weldon Owen Inc.
Reprinted in 1997; 1997; 1998
All rights reserved, including the right of reproduction in whole or in part in any form.

Library of Congress
Cataloging-in-Publication Data:

Carroll, John Phillip.
    Outdoor cooking / general editor, Chuck Williams ;
recipes, John Phillip Carroll ; photography, Allan Rosenberg.
        p.   cm. — (Williams-Sonoma kitchen library)
    Includes index.
    ISBN 0-7835-0320-2
    1. Barbecue cookery.   I. Williams, Chuck.   II. Title.
III. Series.
TX840.B3C3724   1997
641.5'784—dc20   96-24078
                                 CIP

Contents

Introduction 4   Equipment 6   Outdoor Grills 8
Building a Fire 10   Enhancing Flavor 11   Basic Recipes 11

FISH & SHELLFISH 15

POULTRY 29

BEEF, PORK & LAMB 53

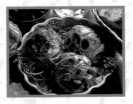

FRUITS, VEGETABLES & SIDE DISHES 83

Glossary 104   Acknowledgments 108   Index 108

INTRODUCTION

We've entered a new era in the way we cook outdoors. Gone are the days when you'd just build a fire in a backyard barbecue, slap on a hamburger or steak, turn it once to get those authentic grill marks on both sides, and then call out, "Come and get it!"

Adventurous cooks have learned that, with a little attention to detail, you can cook almost the same things outdoors that you'd regularly cook on a stove top or in an oven. Thus, you can enjoy the pleasures of preparing food in the open air and savor the added flavor that the smoke of a live fire can contribute.

This book dedicates itself to the many ways you can cook outdoors, from quick grilling of small or thin items to the slow, covered roasting of whole poultry or large cuts of meat over a fire specially built to provide indirect heat akin to that of an oven. On the following pages, you'll find detailed discussions of everything you need, from grills themselves, to tools and accessories, to fuel and sources of fragrant smoke. You'll also learn how to build different kinds of fires to suit different cooking methods, and how various marinades, bastes and sauces can enhance flavor. Following this introductory section are 45 recipes for an incredible variety of outdoor dishes from appetizers to desserts.

I urge you, at the earliest opportunity, to cook your way through the recipes in this book, because each one—in the way its seasonings and techniques suit the featured ingredients—offers its own unique lesson. Prepare a few meals in the open air and you'll soon, most pleasurably, become an expert in outdoor cooking.

Chuck Williams

EQUIPMENT

Straightforward cookware and kitchen tools help you prepare for the simple art of outdoor cooking

Outdoor cooking is so easy that you need very little in the way of special equipment, apart from the grills themselves and a few attendant tools (pages 8–9). The kitchenware shown here is used primarily for the preliminary preparation of food, from cutting up ingredients to making sauces and bastes to marinating.

Two common essentials do not appear here, however. Paper towels are needed to pat foods dry after marinating and before putting them on the grill, thus preventing flare-ups and blackened meat. Large, lock-top plastic bags are good for holding big cuts of meat or poultry while they marinate.

1. Food Processor
Equipped with metal blade for finely chopping and combining marinade and relish ingredients.

2. Colander
For all-purpose rinsing and draining of vegetables, fruits and other ingredients. Choose a sturdy model in stainless steel, shown here, or enameled steel.

3. Saucepan
For simmering sauces. Select a good-quality, heavy saucepan that absorbs and transfers heat well. Anodized aluminum, shown here, or stainless or enameled steel, cleans easily and does not react with acidic ingredients such as wine, citrus juice or tomatoes.

4. Oven Mitt
Made of heavy, quilted cotton for good protection from heat.

5. Cutting Board
Choose one of hardwood or tough but resilient white acrylic. Thoroughly clean the surface after every use.

6. Paring Knife
For trimming and peeling vegetables and cutting up small ingredients.

7. Large Chef's Knife
An all-purpose knife for chopping and slicing vegetables, large items or large quantities of ingredients.

8. Slicing Knife
Long, sturdy but flexible blade easily slices through larger cuts of meat or poultry for serving.

9. Zester
Small, sharp holes at end of stainless-steel blade cut citrus zest in fine shreds.

10. Vegetable Peeler
Curved, slotted blade thinly strips away vegetable peels. Choose a sturdy model that feels comfortable in your hand.

11. Kitchen String
For trussing chickens and other large or unwieldy pieces of food, such as roasts, to give them a compact, even shape for outdoor cooking; and for securing bacon wrapped around poultry or seafood for the grill. Choose good-quality linen string, which withstands intense heat with minimal charring.

12. Bamboo Skewers
For holding small pieces of food to be grilled. Before using, soak bamboo skewers in water for 30 minutes to prevent burning.

13. Kitchen Scissors
Sharp, sturdy scissors for cutting up poultry and other heavy-duty kitchen cutting purposes.

14. Instant-Read Thermometer
Used to provide a quick and accurate assessment of doneness when inserted into a large cut of meat or whole poultry.

15. Citrus Reamer
For quick, easy extraction of juice from halves of lemon or other citrus fruits.

16. Basting Brush
For basting foods with marinades and sauces before and during cooking. Choose a sturdy brush with well-attached natural bristles.

17. Wire Whisk
For briskly mixing marinades and sauces.

18. Mixing Bowls
Sturdy bowls in a wide range of sizes for mixing marinades, spice rubs and sauces; holding cut-up ingredients, seasonings and liquids before cooking; and for soaking wood chips and herbs, loose or in bags, for the fire. Can be made of porcelain, earthenware, glass or stainless steel.

19. Box Grater/Shredder
Sturdy stainless-steel tool for grating or shredding citrus zest, whole ginger or other ingredients by hand.

20. Frying Pan
For general sautéing of ingredients and simmering of sauces. Choose good-quality, heavy stainless steel, thick anodized aluminum or heavy enamel, all of which are nonreactive and conduct and hold heat well. The bottom of a heavy frying pan may also be used for crushing whole peppercorns.

21. Glass Storage Containers
Shallow nonreactive dishes with airtight covers for storing sauces and marinades.

22. Shallow Glass Dish
Large, shallow nonreactive dish for holding food while it marinates.

23. Wooden Spoons and Rubber Spatula
Sturdy implements in a range of sizes and shapes for all-purpose stirring, blending and scraping.

Outdoor Grills

The dizzying array of outdoor cooking equipment for sale in hardware, cookware and specialty stores today might well lead you to believe that there are many different ways to grill outdoors. In general, though, there are only two—direct heat and indirect heat (see page 10)—and both methods can be achieved to some degree with almost any outdoor grill available.

The differences you see come down simply to matters of size, sturdiness and durability, type of fuel, and optional features—all of which will affect the cost of the product you choose.

The smallest outdoor grills, such as square or rectangular Japanese-style hibachis, can be very inexpensive. Bear in mind, however, that they will limit the quantity and size of the foods you cook, with the smallest ones not offering sufficient area to accommodate indirect-heat cooking. They are also often made of cheaper materials that will not last beyond one summer.

Larger, sturdier grills, on the other hand, will accommodate enough burgers or sausages to feed a crowd and are commonly designed to handle the cooking of a large cut of meat or whole poultry by indirect heat. They will last season after season if properly sheltered from the elements when not in use. Some of the largest models, both charcoal and gas fueled, may even be built into brick or stone bases to become permanent patio features.

Charcoal Grills

Consisting simply of a metal pan that holds a bed of glowing charcoal beneath a metal rack, charcoal grills come in many shapes and sizes. These include the small, inexpensive, cast-iron Japanese hibachi; the flat-bottomed brazier, which starred in so many backyard barbecues in the 1950s; and the kettle (below, left), whose spherical shape ensures a high level of fuel efficiency and heat intensity.

Gas Grills

Whether fueled by a natural gas line run from the house or by propane in refillable tanks, the flames of a gas grill (below) burn beneath a bed of heat-absorbent crushed lava rock or ceramic bricks, which in turn cook food placed on the rack above them. More sophisticated models include multiple controls, allowing only parts of the bed to be heated for indirect-heat cooking; separate burners for cooking sauces or heating griddles; and built-in metal boxes that hold and heat wood chips for smoking.

GRILLING ACCESSORIES

Considering the unique characteristics of outdoor grills—the live flames, intense temperatures and, usually, large cooking area—specialized grilling accessories make outdoor cooking both easier and safer. Reasonably priced and widely available, such tools are well worth assembling before you cook outdoors for the first time.

Specialty Grids and Grilling Baskets. For most outdoor cooking purposes, your grill's standard cooking grid will suffice. Some foods, however, may be more easily cooked and turned without falling apart or falling into the fire if you use a specialty grid. Two-sided, hinged and latched baskets, such as the one shown here, enclose burgers, large steaks, seafood or other delicate or hard-to-handle items. Grids composed of fine mesh or of sturdy metal punched with holes let the heat through to cook especially delicate or small items.

Long-Handled Cooking Tools. Utensils with long handles, such as the basting brush, spatula, two-pronged fork and tongs shown here, let you baste, turn and move foods on the grill without risk of exposing your hands or arms to the heat. An extra pair of long-handled tongs is especially useful for rearranging hot coals.

Fire Control and Protection. Keep close at hand an adjustable sprayer filled with water, for quick dousing of fire flare-ups. An oven mitt and pot holder made of heavy, quilted cotton, with one side treated for fire resistance, will protect your hands from intense heat during cooking.

Miscellaneous Accessories. Several items, although not essential, will make outdoor cooking even easier. A flashlight with a high-intensity beam, for example, helps you see what you're cooking after dark. A large, heavy-duty apron guards clothing from splatters. And a good-sized basket made of wicker or other material conveniently and efficiently keeps and holds all your outdoor cooking accessories together in one place.

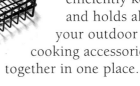

Building a Fire

The most important thing to remember about building a fire for outdoor cooking is to allow yourself enough time for the fire to grow hot. If you are using a charcoal grill, the coals need 25–30 minutes from the time you light them to be ready for cooking: evenly covered in light gray ash or, at night, glowing red. Even gas grills, however, require lighting 10–15 minutes in advance so that their lava-rock or ceramic-brick beds can heat up fully.

Properly building a charcoal fire ensures quick, even burning. Gather coals together in a compact pyramid, burying beneath them paraffin-saturated corn cobs or other fuel-soaked starting aids that can be ignited to start the fire. (Avoid unpleasant fumes by not using lighter fluid, or charcoal that has been pre-saturated with it.) Alternatively, try an efficient, inexpensive chimney fire starter: Load charcoal into the top of the vented metal cylinder, loosely stuff newspaper into the bottom, and then ignite the newspaper with matches or a spark lighter; the coals will be ready in as little as 20 minutes.

Once ready, spread out the coals as needed for direct- or indirect-heat cooking. Adjust the grill's air vents as suggested in specific recipes to regulate the heat. Take care to check food during cooking as the heat of the fire will affect cooking time. Keep a spray bottle of water on hand to douse any flare-ups caused by fat dripping onto the coals.

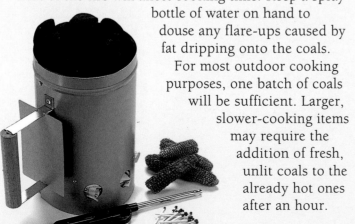

For most outdoor cooking purposes, one batch of coals will be sufficient. Larger, slower-cooking items may require the addition of fresh, unlit coals to the already hot ones after an hour.

Direct Heat

Smaller or thinner food items—some poultry pieces, steaks, burgers, fish fillets—cook quickly via direct heat. Use a long poker, long-handled tongs or another safe tool to spread the hot coals in an even bed directly beneath the rack area to be used for cooking.

Indirect Heat

Think of indirect-heat cooking as similar to roasting in an oven, used for longer, slower cooking of larger pieces of food. Once the coals are hot, spread them in a compact area away from the portion of the rack on which the food will be placed. Here, for a round kettle grill, the coals have been evenly spread around the perimeter. If you wish, place a steel pie plate or pan beneath the cooking area to catch drips. Then close the grill's lid to contain the heat.

ENHANCING FLAVOR

Outdoor cooking offers many simple yet creative opportunities to enhance the flavor of food, including aromatic smoke, sauces and marinades.

SMOKE

Cooking on a grill itself contributes some flavor in the form of smoke that rises from small flare-ups, as fat and juices drip into the fire. More flavor still can be added through the smoke from aromatic wood chips or twigs, as well as from dried herbs scattered loose over the coals or packaged in special bags.

Choose aromatic additions to complement food as you would choose spices or herbs. Mesquite, hickory, alder, apple and pecan woods, as well as grapevine trimmings, add hints of rich, sweet flavor. Woody herbs such as rosemary, oregano and thyme also contribute their familiar flavors.

Before use, soak wood chips or herbs in water for about 1 hour. Drain well and add to the coals while the food cooks. For gas grills, look for small, vented metal smoker boxes into which the soaked aromatics may be put for placing directly on the lava rocks or ceramic bricks.

SAUCES AND MARINADES

Marinades allow food to absorb their flavors before cooking; both marinades and sauces also contribute flavor when basted onto food while it cooks. (Be sure to stop basting meat, poultry or seafood with reserved marinades at least 5 minutes before cooking ends, to avoid possible contamination.)

Midwestern Barbecue Sauce

The Midwest abounds with thick tomato-based barbecue sauces that are a touch hot and sweet, and wonderful on pork ribs, beef brisket or chicken. Because the sauces contain sugar and thus can burn easily, they are usually brushed on during the last 15–20 minutes of cooking. This is also a good dipping sauce to pass at the table.

2 tablespoons vegetable oil
1 yellow onion, chopped
½ cup (2½ oz/75 g) finely chopped celery
1¼ cups (10 fl oz/310 ml) catsup
½ cup (4 fl oz/125 ml) cider vinegar
½ cup (4 fl oz/125 ml) water
⅓ cup (3 oz/90 g) sugar
½ teaspoon cayenne pepper
½ teaspoon salt

*I*n a saucepan over medium-high heat, warm the oil. When hot, add the onion and celery and cook, stirring, until the vegetables have softened, about 7 minutes.

Add the catsup, vinegar, water, sugar, cayenne and salt and stir well. Bring to a boil, then reduce the heat to low, cover partially and simmer until the sauce has thickened slightly, 15–20 minutes.

Remove from the heat and let cool. Use immediately, or transfer to a container, cover tightly and refrigerate for up to 5 days.

Makes about 2¼ cups (18 fl oz/560 ml), enough for 5–6 lb (2.5–3 kg) meat or poultry

Red or White Wine Barbecue Sauce

You can use this herbal, wine-based mixture as a marinade or a baste for chicken, pork, lamb or beef.

1½ cups (12 fl oz/375 ml) dry red or white wine
½ cup (4 fl oz/125 ml) red or white wine vinegar
⅓ cup (3 fl oz/80 ml) olive oil
1 yellow onion, finely chopped
2 tablespoons Worcestershire sauce
2 tablespoons chopped fresh rosemary or thyme, or
   2 teaspoons dried rosemary or thyme
2 teaspoons finely grated lemon zest
½ teaspoon salt
pinch of red pepper flakes

*I*n a saucepan over high heat, combine the wine, wine vinegar, olive oil, onion, Worcestershire sauce, rosemary or thyme, lemon zest, salt and pepper flakes. Bring to a boil, stirring once or twice to combine the ingredients. Reduce the heat to low, cover partially and simmer until the onion has wilted and the sauce has reduced slightly, about 15 minutes.

Remove from the heat and let cool. Use immediately; or transfer to a container, cover tightly and refrigerate for up to 4 days.

Makes about 2 cups (16 fl oz/500 ml),
enough for about 4 lb (2 kg)
meat or poultry

Spicy Mop Sauce

This flavorful concoction belongs to the family of vinegar-based Carolina mop sauces, so-called because they are popular in North and South Carolina and are traditionally swabbed over a slab of meat with an old-fashioned string mop. The sauces vary from sweet and tangy to fiery hot. This one is at once a dash sweet and moderately hot, but you can adjust the amount of sugar and pepper to suit your taste. It's a great marinade for beef, pork or chicken.

1 teaspoon peppercorns
1¼ cups (10 fl oz/310 ml) cider vinegar
⅔ cup (5 fl oz/160 ml) water
3 tablespoons sugar
½ teaspoon salt
1 teaspoon red pepper flakes

*P*lace the peppercorns on a work surface and crush them coarsely by firmly pressing and rolling the bottom of a heavy frying pan or saucepan over them.

In a nonaluminum saucepan over high heat, combine the crushed peppercorns, vinegar, water, sugar, salt and pepper flakes. Bring to a boil, stirring once or twice. Remove from the heat and let stand, uncovered, for at least 1 hour before using, to allow the flavors to blend. For longer storage, let cool completely, then transfer to a non-aluminum container, cover tightly and refrigerate for up to 1 week.

Makes about 2 cups
(16 fl oz/500 ml), enough
for about 4 lb (2 kg)
meat or poultry

Soy-Ginger Marinade

Here, soy sauce, sherry and ginger are combined to make an American version of Japanese teriyaki marinade, which is good on flank steak, skirt steak, chicken, pork and firm-fleshed fish. Marinate steaks, chops or chicken in the refrigerator for at least 3 hours, or up to all day if you wish; marinate fish fillets for 1–2 hours. Large pieces of meat or poultry can marinate for a day or two.

½ cup (4 fl oz/125 ml) soy sauce
½ cup (4 fl oz/125 ml) dry sherry
⅓ cup (3 fl oz/80 ml) vegetable oil
2 tablespoons sugar
2 cloves garlic, minced
1 tablespoon peeled and grated fresh ginger

In a small bowl, combine the soy sauce, sherry, vegetable oil, sugar, garlic and ginger. Whisk until blended. If possible, let stand at room temperature for about 1 hour before using, to allow the flavors to blend.

Makes about 1⅓ cups (11 fl oz/330 ml), enough for about 3 lb (1.5 kg) meat, fish or poultry

Peanut Dipping Sauce

Slightly sweet and slightly hot, this Asian-influenced dipping sauce complements grilled pork or poultry right from the fire. It is also good with firm-fleshed fish, such as swordfish, and on cold chicken or turkey. Pass it in a bowl at the table.

½ cup (4 fl oz/125 ml) water
1 teaspoon cornstarch (cornflour)
½ cup (5 oz/155 g) smooth or chunky peanut butter
¼ cup (2 fl oz/60 ml) fresh lime juice
⅓ cup (3 fl oz/80 ml) soy sauce
¼ cup (2 fl oz/60 ml) Asian sesame oil
2–3 tablespoons sugar
½–1 teaspoon red pepper flakes
¼ teaspoon hot chili oil
¼ cup (⅓ oz/10 g) chopped fresh cilantro
   (fresh coriander)
¼ cup (¾ oz/20 g) chopped green (spring) onion

In a saucepan, combine the water and cornstarch and stir until the cornstarch has dissolved. Add the peanut butter, lime juice, soy sauce, sesame oil, sugar, pepper flakes and chili oil and whisk until smooth. Bring to a boil over medium-high heat, whisking frequently. Reduce the heat to low and simmer, uncovered, until the sauce has thickened slightly, about 3 minutes.

Remove from the heat and let cool. Stir in the cilantro and green onion. Use immediately, or transfer to a container, cover tightly and refrigerate for up to 3 days.

Makes about 1¾ cups (14 fl oz/440 ml); serves 8–10

Halibut with Grilled Pipérade

FOR THE PIPÉRADE:

1 large yellow or red (Spanish) onion,
  cut crosswise into slices ½ inch
  (12 mm) thick
1 red bell pepper (capsicum), seeded,
  deribbed and cut crosswise into rings
  ½ inch (12 mm) thick
1 green bell pepper (capsicum), seeded,
  deribbed and cut crosswise into rings
  ½ inch (12 mm) thick
¼ cup (2 fl oz/60 ml) olive oil
salt to taste, plus ½ teaspoon salt
freshly ground pepper
2 tablespoons chopped fresh thyme or
  1 teaspoon dried thyme
2 tablespoons chopped fresh parsley

FOR THE FISH:

4 halibut fillets, 6–8 oz (185–250 g)
  each and about 1 inch (2.5 cm) thick
4 teaspoons olive oil
salt and freshly ground pepper

Pipérade is a relishlike mixture of cooked vegetables from the Basque region of southern France. It is especially good with grilled tuna, swordfish and chicken breasts, providing both garden-fresh color and flavor.

Prepare a fire for direct-heat cooking in a grill (see page 10). Position the grill rack 4–6 inches (10–15 cm) above the fire.

  To prepare the pipérade, arrange the onion slices and bell pepper rings on the rack. Brush lightly with some of the olive oil and sprinkle with salt and pepper to taste. Grill for about 4 minutes, then turn and again brush lightly with oil. Continue to grill until lightly browned, about 4 minutes longer. Transfer the vegetables to a large bowl and add the ½ teaspoon salt, the thyme and parsley. Toss with a fork to combine—the onion will separate into rings— then set aside while you proceed immediately with the fish.

  To prepare the fish, rub the fillets lightly with the olive oil and sprinkle to taste with salt and pepper. Arrange on the rack. Grill, turning once, until the fillets are lightly browned and opaque throughout, about 10 minutes total.

  To serve, spread the pipérade on a warmed platter or individual plates and arrange the fish on top. Serve immediately.

Serves 4

Tea-Smoked Shrimp with Sweet-and-Hot Pepper Relish

FOR THE RELISH:

¾ cup (4 oz/125 g) chopped green bell
    pepper (capsicum)

¾ cup (4 oz/125 g) chopped red bell
    pepper (capsicum)

½ cup (2 oz/60 g) chopped red (Spanish)
    onion

¼ cup (2 fl oz/60 ml) cider vinegar

1 tablespoon sugar

1 teaspoon mustard seeds

½ teaspoon celery seeds

½ teaspoon salt

⅛ teaspoon cayenne pepper

FOR THE SHRIMP:

2 black or green tea bags

2 lb (1 kg) large or jumbo shrimp
    (prawns), peeled with tails intact,
    deveined and patted dry

3 tablespoons olive oil

½ teaspoon salt

¼ teaspoon freshly ground pepper

Tea bags, soaked in water and then tossed on the hot coals, create an aromatic smoke in much the same way hickory chips do. Tea smoke is much milder, however, and therefore well suited to the delicate taste of fish and shellfish.

*T*o prepare the relish, in a small bowl, combine the green and red peppers and the onion. In a small saucepan over high heat, combine the vinegar, sugar, mustard seeds, celery seeds, salt and cayenne pepper. Bring just to a boil, then pour over the pepper-onion mixture and stir to combine. Let cool, cover and refrigerate for at least 2 hours or for up to 2 days before serving.

Prepare a fire for direct-heat cooking in a grill (see page 10). Position the grill rack 4–6 inches (10–15 cm) above the fire.

To prepare the shrimp, soak the tea bags in cold water to cover for 10–15 minutes. In a large bowl, toss together the shrimp, olive oil, salt and pepper.

Using your hand, squeeze the tea bags to remove any excess water, then drop them onto the fire. Arrange the shrimp on the rack. Cover the grill, open the vents halfway and cook for about 3 minutes. Turn over the shrimp, re-cover and cook until lightly browned and opaque throughout, 3–4 minutes longer.

To serve, transfer the shrimp to a warmed platter or individual plates and serve at once. Pass the relish at the table.

Serves 4–6

Tuna with Beet Relish

FOR THE BEET RELISH:

2 large beets

½ lemon, cut into chunks and seeds
    removed

1 piece fresh ginger, 3–4 inches
    (7.5–10 cm) long, peeled and
    thinly sliced

½ cup (4 oz/125 g) sugar

¼ cup (⅓ oz/10 g) chopped fresh
    parsley

FOR THE FISH:

4 tuna steaks, 6–8 oz (185–250 g) each
    and about 1 inch (2.5 cm) thick

2 tablespoons olive oil or vegetable oil

salt and freshly ground pepper

lemon wedges

Cooked beet relish is reminiscent of a gingery, sweet-hot chutney. Its flavor is a good match for turkey or pork, too.

To prepare the beet relish, trim off the stems from the beets, leaving ½ inch (12 mm) intact; do not peel. Place the beets in a saucepan, add water to cover and bring to a boil. Reduce the heat to low, cover and simmer until tender when pierced, 30–40 minutes. Drain and, when cool enough to handle, cut off the stems and root ends and peel off the skins. Cut into large chunks and let cool.

In a food processor fitted with the metal blade, combine the lemon and ginger and process until finely chopped. Scrape the mixture into a saucepan. Add the beets to the food processor, process to chop coarsely and add them to the saucepan. Stir in the sugar.

Place the saucepan over medium heat and cook, stirring constantly, until the sugar has dissolved and the mixture has thickened slightly, about 4 minutes. Stir in the parsley. Transfer to a bowl to cool; cover and refrigerate until serving.

Prepare a fire for direct-heat cooking in a grill (see page 10). Position the grill rack 4–6 inches (10–15 cm) above the fire.

To prepare the fish, pat dry with paper towels. Rub the steaks on both sides with the oil and sprinkle to taste with salt and pepper. Arrange the fish on the rack. Grill, turning once or twice, until the steaks are lightly browned and opaque throughout, 8–10 minutes.

To serve, transfer to a warmed platter or individual plates. Place a spoonful of relish on each piece of fish and garnish with lemon wedges.

Serves 4

Shrimp and Mushroom Skewers

2 large lemons
18 large or jumbo shrimp (prawns),
    about 1 lb (500 g) total weight
½ cup (4 fl oz/125 ml) olive oil
¼ cup (2 fl oz/60 ml) dry white wine
1 tablespoon chopped fresh thyme or
    1 teaspoon dried thyme, plus thyme
    sprigs for garnish
¾ teaspoon salt
¼ teaspoon freshly ground pepper
18 large fresh white mushrooms, about
    1 lb (500 g) total weight, brushed
    clean and stems removed

The grilled lemon slices have a mildly bitter flavor that pairs nicely with grilled shrimp. If you want to toss an aromatic wood on the fire, use a subtle one such as applewood or grapevine cuttings. Serve the skewers atop cooked polenta or orzo.

Using a sharp knife, cut the lemons into 18 slices about ⅛ inch (3 mm) thick. Save the ends for another use. Using the tip of the knife, pry out any seeds in the slices. Peel and devein the shrimp. Set the lemon slices and shrimp aside.

In a large nonaluminum bowl, whisk together the olive oil, wine, thyme, salt and pepper. Add the lemon slices and shrimp and toss to coat evenly. Cover and refrigerate, tossing once or twice, for about 45 minutes.

Prepare a fire for direct-heat cooking in a grill (see page 10). Position the grill rack 4–6 inches (10–15 cm) above the fire.

Add the mushrooms to the lemons and shrimp and again toss to coat. Let stand for 10–15 minutes.

Thread the shrimp, lemon slices and mushrooms onto skewers in the following manner: Place a lemon slice against the inside curve of a shrimp. Bend the shrimp in half, so that the head end nearly touches the tail end, enclosing the lemon slice in the center. Insert a skewer just above the tail, so that it passes through the body twice. Next, slip a mushroom onto the skewer. Repeat until all the ingredients are used, loading 6 skewers in all. Reserve the remaining marinade.

Arrange the skewers on the rack. Grill, turning frequently and brushing once after 3 minutes with the reserved marinade, until the shrimp have turned pink and the mushrooms are tender and lightly browned, 8–10 minutes total.

Transfer to a warmed platter and garnish with thyme sprigs.

Serves 4–6

Thai-Style Swordfish with Lime and Cilantro Sauce

FOR THE SAUCE:
½ small fresh jalapeño chili pepper
⅓ cup (⅓ oz/10 g) chopped fresh
   cilantro (fresh coriander)
¼ cup (2 fl oz/60 ml) fresh lime juice
2 cloves garlic, minced
2 tablespoons vegetable oil
½ teaspoon salt

FOR THE FISH:
4 swordfish steaks, 6–8 oz (185–250 g)
   each and about 1 inch (2.5 cm) thick
2 tablespoons vegetable oil
salt and freshly ground pepper

Firm-textured and sturdy, swordfish is perfect for outdoor cooking because it doesn't fall apart on the grill. This spry sauce enlivens the mild-flavored fish.

To prepare the sauce, remove any seeds and ribs from the chili pepper half, then finely mince it. In a small bowl, combine the minced pepper, cilantro, lime juice, garlic, vegetable oil and salt. Stir with a fork to combine, then cover and refrigerate for at least 2 hours, or for up to 2 days before serving.

Prepare a fire for direct-heat cooking in a grill (see page 10). Position the grill rack 4–6 inches (10–15 cm) above the fire.

To prepare the fish, rub the steaks on both sides with the vegetable oil and sprinkle to taste with salt and pepper.

Arrange the fish on the rack. Grill, turning once or twice, until the steaks are well browned on both sides and opaque throughout, about 10 minutes.

To serve, transfer to a warmed platter or individual plates. Place a small spoonful of sauce on each piece of fish and serve at once. Pass the remaining sauce at the table.

Serves 4

Bacon-Wrapped Scallop and Salmon Skewers

8 slices bacon, about ½ lb (250 g), cut
   into 3-inch (7.5-cm) lengths
1 lb (500 g) skinless salmon fillets,
   about 1 inch (2.5 cm) thick
1 lb (500 g) sea scallops
¼ cup (2 fl oz/60 ml) olive oil
2 tablespoons fresh lemon juice
2 tablespoons chopped fresh sage or
   1 teaspoon dried sage
½ teaspoon salt
¼ teaspoon freshly ground pepper

lemon wedges

*Blanching bacon—boiling it briefly in water—removes some of its
fat and salt and tames its smoky flavor.*

Fill a saucepan two-thirds full with water and bring to a boil
over high heat. Add the bacon and blanch for 3 minutes. Drain,
rinse with cold water and pat dry with paper towels. Set aside.

Run your fingers over the salmon fillets to detect any errant
bones; remove and discard any bones you find. Cut the salmon
into 1-inch (2.5-cm) cubes. If the small, flat muscle, or "foot,"
is still attached to the sides of each scallop, use your fingers or
a small, sharp knife to remove and discard it. Place the scallops
in a bowl with the salmon and add the olive oil, lemon juice,
sage, salt and pepper. Toss to combine and coat the fish. Cover
and refrigerate, tossing once or twice, for about 30 minutes.

Prepare a fire for direct-heat cooking in a grill (see page 10).
Position the grill rack 4–6 inches (10–15 cm) above the fire.

Remove the scallops and salmon from the marinade; reserve
the marinade. Wrap a piece of bacon around each scallop and
each piece of salmon. Alternate the bacon-wrapped scallops
and salmon on 4 or 6 skewers.

Arrange the skewers on the rack. Grill, turning frequently
and brushing two or three times during the first 4 minutes of
cooking with the reserved marinade, until the bacon is lightly
browned and sizzling and the scallops and salmon are just
opaque throughout, about 8 minutes total.

To serve, transfer to a warmed platter and serve at once with
lemon wedges.

Serves 4–6

Lemon-Dill Salmon and Asparagus

FOR THE ASPARAGUS:

16–20 large, thick asparagus spears, about 1 lb (500 g) total weight

⅓ cup (3 fl oz/80 ml) olive oil

2 tablespoons fresh lemon juice

2 tablespoons chopped fresh dill or 1 teaspoon dried dill

1 teaspoon salt

¼ teaspoon freshly ground pepper

FOR THE SALMON:

1 whole salmon, cleaned, 3½–4 lb (1.75–2 kg)

3 tablespoons olive oil

salt and freshly ground pepper

1 large lemon, thinly sliced, plus lemon wedges for garnish

1 bunch fresh dill, separated into large sprigs

*T*o prepare the asparagus, remove the tough stem ends. Using a vegetable peeler and starting about 2 inches (5 cm) below the tip, peel off the thin outer skin. Arrange in a shallow nonaluminum dish. In a small bowl, whisk together the oil, lemon juice, dill, salt and pepper. Pour over the asparagus and turn to coat. Set aside for 30–60 minutes, turning once at the halfway point.

Prepare a fire for indirect-heat cooking in a covered grill (see page 10). Position the grill rack 4–6 inches (10–15 cm) above the fire.

To prepare the salmon, rinse with cold water, then pat dry with paper towels. Rub inside and out with the olive oil, then sprinkle liberally with salt and pepper. Place the lemon slices and dill sprigs in the cavity and stitch closed with a long wooden skewer or a trussing needle and kitchen string.

Place the fish on the center of the rack, cover and open the vents halfway. Cook for 15 minutes. Using 1 large metal spatula at each end of the fish, flip the fish to its other side in one smooth movement. Don't worry if some of the skin sticks to the rack.

Remove the asparagus from its marinade and arrange around the fish. Re-cover and cook for about 12 minutes longer, turning the asparagus halfway through cooking. The fish is done when the flesh is opaque throughout and firm to the touch, or an instant-read thermometer inserted into the thickest part registers 140°F (60°C).

Transfer the fish to a warmed platter, arrange the asparagus around it and serve with lemon wedges. Use 2 spatulas or 2 large spoons to remove the fish from its frame in serving-sized pieces.

Serves 6–8

Jamaican Jerk Chicken

8–10 fresh jalapeño chili peppers
¼ cup (2 fl oz/60 ml) fresh lime juice
¼ cup (⅓ oz/10 g) chopped fresh
  rosemary or 1 tablespoon dried
  rosemary, plus rosemary sprigs for
  garnish
2 tablespoons chopped fresh thyme or
  2 teaspoons dried thyme
2 tablespoons mustard seeds
2 tablespoons Dijon-style mustard
½ yellow onion, cut into chunks
2 large cloves garlic
1 teaspoon salt
4–5 lb (2–2.5 kg) chicken pieces

Jerk is a traditional Jamaican style of cooking that begins by rubbing meat or poultry with a pastelike marinade of chili peppers, lime juice, herbs and spices, then grilling it slowly so the marinade forms a coating that seals in the meat juices. If you like your grilled food spicy, this fiery dish is for you.

*H*alve the peppers and remove their stems, seeds and ribs. In a food processor fitted with the metal blade, combine the peppers, lime juice, rosemary, thyme, mustard seeds, mustard, onion, garlic and salt. Process until the mixture forms a thick, smooth paste. If time permits, scrape the paste into a small bowl, cover and refrigerate for about 2 hours, or for up to 2 days before using. This allows the paste to firm up a bit and gives the flavors time to blend.

Pat the chicken dry with paper towels. Rub the chicken pieces with the paste, coating them completely, and place them on a nonaluminum platter or baking sheet. Cover with plastic wrap and refrigerate for at least 2 hours, or for up to 24 hours.

Prepare a fire for indirect-heat cooking in a covered grill (see page 10). Position the grill rack 4–6 inches (10–15 cm) above the fire.

Place the chicken, skin side down, on the center of the rack. Cover the grill and open the vents slightly less than halfway. Have a spray bottle of water handy to douse any flare-ups. Cook slowly, turning the chicken every 15 minutes, until opaque throughout and the juices run clear, 60–70 minutes.

To serve, transfer to a warmed platter or individual plates, garnish with rosemary sprigs and serve at once.

Serves 4–6

Chicken Breasts with Black Olive Butter

FOR THE BLACK OLIVE BUTTER:

½ cup (4 oz/125 g) unsalted butter, at room temperature

¼ cup (1¼ oz/37 g) chopped black olives

2 tablespoons chopped fresh parsley or tarragon

1 tablespoon fresh lemon juice

pinch of freshly ground pepper

FOR THE CHICKEN:

3 boneless whole chicken breasts with the skin intact, 10–12 oz (315–375 g) each

4 teaspoons vegetable oil

salt and freshly ground pepper

To prepare the black olive butter, in a small bowl, combine the butter, olives, parsley or tarragon, lemon juice and pepper. Using a fork or wooden spoon, beat vigorously until blended. Transfer half of the butter mixture to a sheet of plastic wrap and shape it into a log about 3 inches (7.5 cm) long and 1 inch (2.5 cm) in diameter. Wrap in the plastic wrap and chill until firm, at least 1 hour. Set the remaining butter mixture aside.

Prepare a fire for indirect-heat cooking in a covered grill (see page 10). Position the grill rack 4–6 inches (10–15 cm) above the fire.

Working with 1 chicken breast at a time, gently slide your fingertips under the skin to make a pocket. Divide the butter mixture in the bowl into 3 equal portions and, using your fingertips, slip a portion under the skin of each breast, distributing it evenly. Tie pieces of kitchen string crosswise around each breast in 2 places, to make a cylindrical roll. Rub the breasts with the vegetable oil; sprinkle to taste with salt and pepper.

Place the chicken on the center of the rack, cover and open the vents halfway. Cook for 20 minutes. Turn the chicken and continue to cook until browned and opaque throughout, or until an instant-read thermometer inserted into a breast registers 170°F (77°C), about 20 minutes longer. Remove from the grill, cover loosely with aluminum foil and let rest for 5 minutes.

To serve, snip the strings and cut each breast crosswise into slices ½ inch (12 mm) thick. Arrange on warmed individual plates. Cut the butter log into slices and place on top of each serving. Serve at once.

Serves 6

Bacon-Wrapped Cornish Hens

8 slices bacon, about ½ lb (250 g) total
4 Cornish game hens, about 1¼ lb
   (625 g) each
salt and freshly ground pepper
4–8 fresh parsley sprigs
4–8 fresh thyme sprigs

Cornish game hens tend to be dry, but a couple of slices of blanched bacon tied around each bird help to keep it moist and succulent. This recipe is delicious served with ratatouille from the grill (recipe on page 84).

Prepare a fire for indirect-heat cooking in a covered grill (see page 10). Position the grill rack 4–6 inches (10–15 cm) above the fire.

Fill a large saucepan two-thirds full with water and bring to a boil over high heat. Add the bacon and blanch for 3 minutes. Drain, then rinse the bacon with cold water and pat dry with paper towels. Set aside.

Pat the hens dry with paper towels. Sprinkle them inside and out with salt and pepper to taste. Tuck a sprig or two of parsley and thyme into each body cavity. Crisscross 2 slices of bacon across the breast of each hen. Using kitchen string, tie the bacon securely to the birds.

Place the hens, breast side up, on the center of the rack. Cover the grill and open the vents halfway. Cook for 30 minutes, then turn breast side down. Continue cooking in the covered grill until the birds are well browned, opaque throughout and the juices run clear, or until an instant-read thermometer inserted into the thickest part of a breast registers 170°F (77°C) or inserted into the thickest part of a thigh registers 185°F (85°C), 20–25 minutes longer.

To serve, snip the strings and arrange the birds on a warmed platter or individual plates with the bacon alongside.

Serves 4

Orange-Roasted Duck

1 cup (8 fl oz/250 ml) fresh orange juice
½ cup (4 fl oz/125 ml) dry white
  vermouth
¼ cup (2½ oz/75 g) orange marmalade
1 tablespoon chopped fresh thyme or
  1 teaspoon dried thyme
½ teaspoon salt
1 bone-in whole duck breast, 1¼–1½ lb
  (625–750 g)

The easiest cut of duck to grill is a bone-in breast because it isn't as fat-laden as other parts of the bird. This orange-infused duck breast makes an elegant meal for two. Serve with puréed parsnips or celeriac (celery root) and a green vegetable.

*I*n a small bowl, whisk together the orange juice, vermouth, marmalade, thyme and salt. Using a sharp knife, score the duck skin with several crisscross diagonal cuts about ¼ inch (6 mm) deep. Place the duck breast in a shallow nonaluminum dish large enough for it to lie flat. Pour the marinade over the breast and turn to coat both sides. Cover and refrigerate, turning occasionally, for at least 1 hour, or all day if you wish.

Prepare a fire for direct-heat cooking in a grill (see page 10). Position the grill rack 4–6 inches (10–15 cm) above the fire.

Remove the duck from the marinade and pat dry with paper towels; reserve the marinade.

Place the duck on the rack. Have a spray bottle of water handy to douse flare-ups. Grill, turning frequently and brushing three or four times with the reserved marinade, until the skin is well browned and the meat is still slightly pink at the bone, 18–20 minutes. For medium to well done, grill an additional 5–7 minutes. Stop brushing with the marinade 5 minutes before the duck is done.

Remove the duck from the grill, cover loosely with aluminum foil and let rest for 5 minutes. To serve, cut the meat from the bone into thin slices and arrange on warmed individual plates. If you wish, remove the crispy skin, cut into thin strips and serve with the meat.

Serves 2

Turkey Kabobs with Peanut Dipping Sauce

1 skinless, boneless turkey breast,
  2 lb (1 kg)
½ cup (4 fl oz/125 ml) dry white wine
¼ cup (2 fl oz/60 ml) soy sauce
¼ cup (2 fl oz/60 ml) vegetable oil or
  olive oil
1 tablespoon sugar
1 large clove garlic, minced
½ teaspoon freshly ground pepper

peanut dipping sauce (*recipe on page 13*)

Skewers of turkey breast meat are easy to cook even on a small grill. Serve over steamed or fried rice and accompany with the peanut dipping sauce.

Cut the turkey breast into 1½-inch (4-cm) cubes. In a large bowl, whisk together the wine, soy sauce, oil, sugar, garlic and pepper. Add the turkey and toss to coat evenly. Cover and refrigerate, tossing occasionally, for at least 3 hours, or all day if you wish.

Prepare a fire for direct-heat cooking in a grill (see page 10). Position the grill rack 4–6 inches (10–15 cm) above the fire.

Remove the turkey from the marinade and pat dry with paper towels; reserve the marinade. Thread the turkey onto 4 or 6 skewers.

Arrange the skewers on the rack. Grill, turning frequently and brushing occasionally with the reserved marinade, until the turkey is no longer pink in the center, about 20 minutes. Stop brushing with the marinade 5 minutes before the turkey is done.

To serve, transfer to warmed individual plates and serve immediately with the peanut sauce.

Serves 4–6

Tropical Chicken Breasts

1 cup (6 oz/185 g) fresh pineapple
   chunks or drained, canned
   unsweetened pineapple chunks
⅔ cup (5 fl oz/160 ml) canned coconut
   milk
1 piece fresh ginger, 4–5 inches (10–13
   cm) long, peeled and thinly sliced
½ teaspoon salt
¼ teaspoon freshly ground pepper
6 skinless, boneless chicken breast
   halves, 4–6 oz (125–185 g) each

*A ginger-coconut marinade infuses these chicken breasts with
rich flavor and then forms a sweet glaze as the meat cooks
on the grill.*

*I*n a blender or a food processor fitted with the metal
blade, combine the pineapple, coconut milk, ginger, salt
and pepper and process until smooth.

Arrange the chicken breasts in a single layer in a shallow
nonaluminum dish. Pour the pineapple mixture over the
chicken and turn to coat evenly. Cover and let marinate in
the refrigerator for 2–3 hours.

Prepare a fire for direct-heat cooking in a grill (see page 10).
Position the grill rack 4–6 inches (10–15 cm) above the fire.

Remove the chicken breasts from the marinade; reserve
the marinade.

Arrange the chicken on the rack and grill for 5 minutes.
Brush with the reserved marinade, turn over the chicken,
and grill for 5 minutes longer. Again brush with the marinade and turn over. Continue cooking until the chicken is
browned outside, opaque throughout and the juices run
clear, 5–10 minutes longer.

To serve, transfer to warmed individual plates and serve
immediately.

Serves 6

Deviled Chicken

1 frying chicken, 3½–4 lb (1.75–2 kg)

spicy mop sauce (*recipe on page 12*)

¼ cup (2 oz/60 g) Dijon-style mustard

2 tablespoons minced shallots or green (spring) onions

¼ teaspoon cayenne pepper

1 cup (2 oz/60 g) fresh white bread crumbs

Deviled means the chicken is brushed with mustard and sprinkled with bread crumbs to make a spicy, crunchy coating. You may substitute chicken halves for the whole butterflied bird, if you like.

*F*irst, butterfly the chicken: Place the bird on a work surface, breast side down. Using a sharp knife or heavy-duty kitchen scissors, cut lengthwise down the backbone, slitting the bird from its neck to its tail. Open the chicken as flat as possible and turn skin side up. Using your fist, firmly strike the breastbone to break the ridge of the bone and flatten the breast.

Place the chicken in a shallow nonaluminum dish large enough for it to lie flat. Pour the mop sauce over the chicken and turn to coat both sides. Cover and refrigerate, turning occasionally, for at least 3 hours, or all day if you wish.

Prepare a fire for indirect-heat cooking in a covered grill (see page 10). Position the grill rack 4–6 inches (10–15 cm) above the fire.

In a small bowl, stir together the mustard, shallots or green onions and cayenne; set aside.

Remove the chicken from the marinade and pat it dry with paper towels. Place the chicken, skin side down, on the perimeter of the rack, directly over the coals. Have a spray bottle of water handy to douse flare-ups. Grill uncovered, turning frequently, for about 25 minutes. Move the chicken so it is not directly over the fire, turn it skin side up and brush with the mustard mixture. Sprinkle the crumbs over the mustard and pat them in gently. Cover the grill and open the vents halfway. Cook until the crumbs are crisp and very lightly browned, and the chicken is opaque throughout and its juices run clear, 10–15 minutes longer.

To serve, cut into pieces and arrange on a warmed platter.

Serves 2–4

Turkey Burgers with Apple-Mint Relish

FOR THE APPLE-MINT RELISH:
2 apples, preferably Golden Delicious
¼ cup (2 fl oz/60 ml) cider vinegar
2 tablespoons chopped fresh mint or
    1 teaspoon dried mint
1 tablespoon sugar
1 tablespoon vegetable oil
½ teaspoon celery seeds
½ teaspoon mustard seeds
⅛ teaspoon salt

FOR THE TURKEY BURGERS:
2 lb (1 kg) ground (minced) turkey
1 cup (4 oz/125 g) shredded Cheddar
    cheese
¼ cup (1 oz/30 g) chopped shallots
1 clove garlic, minced
1½ teaspoons salt
½ teaspoon freshly ground pepper

A pleasant change from ground beef burgers, these cheese-laced turkey burgers are complemented by the cool crunch of the apple relish. Serve the burgers on hamburger buns or French rolls, if you wish.

*T*o prepare the relish, peel, halve and core the apples. Chop them finely or, using the large holes of a hand-held grater/shredder, shred them. Transfer to a large bowl and add the vinegar, mint, sugar, oil, celery seeds, mustard seeds and salt. Stir and toss with a fork to combine, then cover and refrigerate for at least 2 hours before serving to blend the flavors and keep the relish crisp.

Prepare a fire for direct-heat cooking in a grill (see page 10). Position the grill rack 4–6 inches (10–15 cm) above the fire.

To prepare the turkey burgers, in a large bowl, combine the turkey, cheese, shallots, garlic, salt and pepper. Using a fork, mix gently to combine. Shape into 6 patties each about 3 inches (7.5 cm) in diameter and 1 inch (2.5 cm) thick.

Place the patties on the rack. Grill, turning two or three times, until the burgers are well browned on both sides and no longer pink in the center, 16–20 minutes.

To serve, transfer to a warmed platter. Pass the relish at the table.

Serves 6

Tandoori Chicken

FOR THE CUCUMBER-YOGURT SAUCE:

1 cucumber

1 cup (8 oz/250 g) plain yogurt

¼ cup (⅓ oz/10 g) chopped fresh cilantro
  (fresh coriander) or mint

½ teaspoon salt

¼ teaspoon freshly ground pepper

FOR THE CHICKEN:

¾ cup (6 oz/185 g) plain yogurt

3 tablespoons fresh lemon juice

4 tablespoons (2 fl oz/60 ml) peanut oil
  or vegetable oil

1 tablespoon minced garlic

1 tablespoon peeled and grated fresh
  ginger

1 tablespoon curry powder

1 teaspoon ground turmeric

1 teaspoon salt

½ teaspoon cayenne pepper

1 frying chicken, 3½–4 lb (1.75–2 kg),
  quartered

Tandoori refers to foods permeated with a yogurt marinade and then cooked in an Indian earthenware oven called a tandoor. You can achieve a similar effect in a covered grill.

*T*o prepare the sauce, peel the cucumber, halve it lengthwise, then scrape out the seeds. Cut the cucumber crosswise into thin slices. In a bowl, stir together the cucumber slices, yogurt, cilantro or mint, salt and pepper. Cover and refrigerate until serving.

To prepare the chicken, in a small bowl, stir together the yogurt, lemon juice, 2 tablespoons of the oil, the garlic, ginger, curry powder, turmeric, salt and cayenne to make a marinade; set aside.

Remove and discard the skin from the chicken. Using a sharp knife, score the chicken meat ½ inch (12 mm) deep at 1-inch (2.5-cm) intervals. Place in a single layer in a shallow non-aluminum dish large enough for the pieces to lie flat. Add the marinade, coating evenly and working it into the cuts. Cover and refrigerate for at least 3 hours, or as long as overnight.

Prepare a fire for direct-heat cooking in a covered grill (see page 10). Position the grill rack 4–6 inches (10–15 cm) above the fire.

Remove the chicken from the marinade. Scrape most of the marinade from the chicken; reserve the marinade. Rub the chicken with the remaining 2 tablespoons oil. Place on the rack. Grill, uncovered, for 10 minutes, then turn and brush with some of the reserved marinade. Grill for 10 minutes more, then again turn and brush with the marinade. Cover the grill, open the vents halfway and cook until the chicken is opaque throughout and the juices run clear, about 15 minutes longer.

To serve, transfer to a warmed platter and serve at once. Pass the cucumber-yogurt sauce at the table.

Serves 4

Hickory-Smoked Turkey Thighs

1½ teaspoons salt
1 teaspoon freshly ground pepper
1 teaspoon dried sage
1 teaspoon dried thyme
finely grated zest of 1 lemon
4 turkey thighs, about 1½ lb (750 g) each
4 teaspoons vegetable oil

Dropping damp hickory chips onto the fire gives turkey a subtle, smoky taste. The dry marinade forms a spicy coating and helps bring out the turkey's natural flavor. Large turkey thighs are easy to cook, and each one makes two generous helpings, so this is a good recipe to double for a crowd. Serve with cranberry sauce or beet relish (recipe on page 19) and potato salad or coleslaw.

Soak a handful (about 2 oz/60 g) of hickory chips in water to cover for at least 1 hour.

To prepare the dry marinade, in a small bowl, stir together the salt, pepper, sage, thyme and lemon zest. Pat the turkey thighs dry with paper towels. Rub them with the vegetable oil, and then rub each one with the marinade. Let stand at room temperature for 1 hour, or cover and refrigerate for several hours.

Prepare a fire for indirect-heat cooking in a covered grill (see page 10). Position the grill rack 4–6 inches (10–15 cm) above the fire. Scoop the hickory chips out of the water and drop them onto the fire.

Place the turkey thighs, skin side down, on the center of the rack. Cover the grill and open the vents halfway. Cook, turning two or three times, until well browned, opaque throughout and the juices run clear, or until an instant-read thermometer inserted into the thickest portion of the thigh registers 185°F (85°C), 50–60 minutes.

Remove from the grill, cut each thigh in half along one side of the bone and arrange on a warmed platter or individual plates. Serve immediately.

Serves 8

Grill-Roasted Chicken with Potato Fans

FOR THE CHICKEN:

1 roasting chicken, 5–6 lb (2.5–3 kg)
1 lemon, halved
salt and freshly ground pepper
several fresh rosemary, thyme, sage or
    parsley sprigs
1–2 tablespoons olive oil or vegetable oil

FOR THE POTATOES:

4 baking potatoes, about ½ lb (250 g)
    each, peeled
3 tablespoons unsalted butter, melted
1 teaspoon salt
½ teaspoon freshly ground pepper

Baking potatoes and a roasting chicken are good grill partners because both cook in the same amount of time.

Prepare a fire for indirect-heat cooking in a covered grill (see page 10). Position the grill rack 4–6 inches (10–15 cm) above the fire.

To prepare the chicken, pat dry with paper towels. Rub inside and outside the chicken with a cut side of the lemon. Sprinkle inside and out with salt and pepper. Tuck the herb sprigs inside the cavity. Rub the skin with the oil. Truss the chicken. Cross the drumsticks and, using kitchen string, tie the legs together, then tie the legs and wings close to the body. Set aside.

To prepare the potatoes, slice each one crosswise at ¼-inch (6-mm) intervals, cutting only three-fourths of the way through; the slices must remain attached. In a large bowl, gently turn the potatoes in the butter. Season with the salt and pepper.

Place the chicken breast-side down on the center of the rack. Place the potatoes cut-side up alongside the bird. Cover the grill and open the vents halfway. After 30 minutes, turn the chicken breast-side up, and turn the potatoes cut-side down. Cook the chicken until the juices run clear when the thigh joint is pierced, or until an instant-read thermometer inserted into the thickest part of the breast registers 170°F (77°C) or into the thickest part of the thigh registers 185°F (85°C), about 1 hour total. The potatoes will be tender in about the same amount of time.

Transfer the chicken to a warmed platter and let rest for 10 minutes; keep the potatoes warm on the grill. To serve, snip the strings and carve the chicken. Arrange the potatoes alongside.

Serves 4

Turkey Sausages with Chutney Mustard

½ cup (4 oz/125 g) whole-grain
  mustard
¼ cup (2½ oz/75 g) mango chutney
¼ cup (⅓ oz/10 g) chopped fresh
  cilantro (fresh coriander)
2 lb (1 kg) turkey sausages

It is important to cook sausages fully. If you like, prick the sausages several times with a fork, then blanch them in simmering water for about 5 minutes before grilling. This removes some of the fat and reduces the tendency toward flare-ups on the fire. Chicken sausages may be substituted. Garnish with slices of fresh mango, if you wish.

Prepare a fire for direct-heat cooking in a grill (see page 10). Position the grill rack 4–6 inches (10–15 cm) above the fire.

In a small bowl, stir together the mustard, chutney and cilantro. Cover and refrigerate until serving.

Arrange the sausages on the rack. Have a spray bottle of water handy to douse flare-ups. Grill, turning every 2 minutes, until the sausages are well browned on the outside and no longer pink in the center, about 15 minutes.

To serve, transfer the sausages to a warmed platter. Pass the chutney mustard at the table.

Serves 4–6

Beef Top Round with Jalapeño Marinade

3 fresh jalapeño chili peppers
⅔ cup (5 fl oz/160 ml) dry red wine
⅓ cup (3 fl oz/80 ml) olive oil
2 large cloves garlic
handful of fresh parsley sprigs
1 teaspoon salt
½ teaspoon freshly ground pepper
1 top round beef steak, about 2½ lb
   (1.25 kg)

Top round is a tasty cut, but you must be careful not to overcook it or its flavor will be lost and its texture will toughen. In the market, this same cut is sometimes labeled London broil. This is delicious accompanied with grilled fennel and endive with olive vinaigrette (recipe on page 91).

*H*alve the peppers and remove their stems, seeds and ribs. In a blender or a food processor fitted with the metal blade, combine the jalapeños, wine, olive oil, garlic, parsley, salt and ground pepper. Process until blended and smooth.

Using a sharp knife, score the surface of the steak with crisscross cuts about ⅛ inch (3 mm) deep and 2 inches (5 cm) apart. Place in a large lock-top plastic bag and pour in the jalapeño mixture. Press out the air and seal the bag tightly. Massage the bag gently to distribute the marinade evenly. Place in a large bowl and refrigerate, turning and massaging the bag occasionally, for at least 6 hours, or for up to a day or two if you wish.

Prepare a fire for direct-heat cooking in a grill (see page 10). Position the grill rack 4–6 inches (10–15 cm) above the fire.

Remove the steak from the marinade and pat it dry with paper towels; reserve the marinade.

Place the steak on the rack. Grill, turning and brushing with the reserved marinade three or four times, until done to your liking, 14–16 minutes for rare or 18–20 minutes for medium.

To serve, carve into thin slices on the diagonal and across the grain. Arrange on a warmed platter and serve at once.

Serves 6

Lamb and Eggplant Burgers

1 large eggplant (aubergine), 3–4 inches (7.5–10 cm) in diameter and 6–7 inches (15–18 cm) long

salt for sprinkling, plus 1½ teaspoons salt

2 lb (1 kg) ground (minced) lamb

½ teaspoon freshly ground pepper

2 cloves garlic, minced

½ cup (4 fl oz/125 ml) olive oil

Eggplant slices replace the buns on these burgers, which are most easily eaten with a knife and fork. Lettuce leaves, tomato slices, raw or grilled onion slices, and mayonnaise flavored with minced garlic are good condiments.

Cover a baking sheet with paper towels. Trim the eggplant and then cut crosswise into slices about ½ inch (12 mm) thick. You should have 12 good-sized slices in all. Sprinkle both sides of each slice lightly with salt. Spread the slices out on the towel-lined baking sheet and cover with more paper towels. Let stand for about 1 hour.

Prepare a fire for direct-heat cooking in a grill (see page 10). Position the grill rack 4–6 inches (10–15 cm) above the fire.

Rinse the eggplant slices and pat them dry with paper towels. Set aside.

In a large bowl, combine the lamb, 1½ teaspoons salt, the pepper and garlic. Mix gently to combine, handling the meat as lightly as possible. Shape the mixture into 6 patties each about 3½ inches (8.5 cm) in diameter and 1 inch (2.5 cm) thick.

Arrange the eggplant slices and the lamb patties on the rack. Grill, turning both the burgers and the eggplant slices every 2–3 minutes, brushing the eggplant slices with the olive oil each time you turn them. Grill the eggplant until lightly browned on both sides, about 8 minutes total. Grill the lamb until done to your liking, about 8 minutes total for rare, 10 minutes for medium or 12 minutes for well done.

To serve, slip each lamb burger between 2 eggplant slices and place on warmed individual plates. Serve at once.

Serves 6

Old-fashioned Rib Roast

4 teaspoons coarse or kosher salt

3 tablespoons chopped fresh thyme
  or 2 teaspoons dried thyme

1½ teaspoons freshly ground pepper

2 large cloves garlic, minced

finely grated zest of 1 lemon or lime

1 beef rib roast, 6–7 lb (3–3.5 kg),
  trimmed of excess fat and tied for
  roasting (*see note*)

2 tablespoons vegetable oil

If you like beef prepared simply, this dish is for you. Serve it with baking potatoes, if you like: Place them on the grill rack around the roast for the last hour or so of cooking. Slow-cooked onions with tarragon mustard sauce (recipe on page 97) also make a good accompaniment. Before cooking, tie the roast at 1-inch (2.5-cm) intervals for roasting, or have the butcher do it for you.

Prepare a fire for indirect-heat cooking in a covered grill (see page 10). Position the grill rack 4–6 inches (10–15 cm) above the fire.

In a small bowl, stir together the salt, thyme, pepper, garlic and lemon or lime zest; set aside.

Pat the roast dry with paper towels. Rub with the vegetable oil, then rub the salt mixture over the surface of the meat.

Place the roast rib-side down on the center of the rack. Cover the grill and open the vents halfway. Cook for 45 minutes. Turn the roast rib-side up and cook until done to your liking, about 45 minutes longer for rare or 55–60 minutes longer for medium, or until an instant-read thermometer inserted into the thickest portion of the roast away from the bone registers 130°F (54°C) for rare and 140°F (60°C) for medium.

Remove the roast from the grill and transfer to a cutting board. Cover loosely with aluminum foil and let rest for 10 minutes. To serve, snip and discard the strings. Carve the meat across the grain into slices ¾–1 inch (2–2.5 cm) thick and arrange on a warmed platter.

Serves 6

All-American Beef Short Ribs

1 cup (8 fl oz/250 ml) unsweetened
pineapple juice
¼ cup (2 fl oz/60 ml) vegetable oil
¼ cup (2 fl oz/60 ml) soy sauce
¼ cup (2 oz/60 g) firmly packed light
brown sugar
1 tablespoon chili powder
4 lb (2 kg) beef short ribs, trimmed of
excess fat
midwestern barbecue sauce (*recipe on
page 11*)

Shorts ribs benefit from long, slow cooking, so that the meat practically falls off the bone. At the table, moisten the ribs with plenty of tangy barbecue sauce.

*I*n a small bowl, whisk together the pineapple juice, vegetable oil, soy sauce, brown sugar and chili powder. Place the ribs in a large lock-top plastic bag and pour in the pineapple mixture. Press out the air and seal the bag tightly. Massage the bag gently to distribute the marinade evenly. Place in a large bowl and refrigerate for at least 4 hours, or for up to 2 days if you wish.

Prepare a fire for indirect-heat cooking in a covered grill (see page 10). Position the grill rack 4–6 inches (10–15 cm) above the fire.

Remove the ribs from the marinade and pat them dry with paper towels. Reserve the marinade.

Place the ribs on the center of the rack, cover the grill and open the vents halfway. Cook for 1 hour, then turn and brush with the reserved marinade. Add a few more coals to the fire if necessary to maintain a constant temperature. Continue to cook, brushing with the marinade and turning every 20–30 minutes, until the meat is well browned and begins to shrink from the bone, 1½–2 hours longer.

To serve, transfer the ribs to a warmed platter or individual plates. Pass the barbecue sauce at the table.

Serves 4

Steak Fajitas

⅓ cup (3 fl oz/80 ml) tequila

¼ cup (2 fl oz/60 ml) fresh lime juice

2 tablespoons vegetable oil

2 cloves garlic, minced

½ teaspoon salt, plus salt to taste

½ teaspoon red pepper flakes

2 lb (1 kg) skirt steak

2 red (Spanish) or yellow onions, cut crosswise into slices ½ inch (12 mm) thick

3 red or green bell peppers (capsicums), seeded, deribbed and cut crosswise into rings ½ inch (12 mm) thick

olive oil or vegetable oil for brushing

12 or more flour tortillas, each 8–10 inches (20–25 cm) in diameter, warmed

tomato salsa, optional

guacamole, optional

sour cream, optional

A casual and tasty meal from the grill, fajitas are traditionally made from skirt steak, but flank steak can also be used. If you use skirt steak, be sure to have your butcher skin it for you. Tuck the flavorful meat strips into flour tortillas warmed briefly on the grill.

In a small bowl, whisk together the tequila, lime juice, vegetable oil, garlic, the ½ teaspoon salt and the pepper flakes. Place the meat in a shallow nonaluminum dish large enough for it to lie flat. Pour the tequila mixture over the steak and turn to coat both sides. Cover and refrigerate, turning occasionally, for at least 3 hours, or all day if you wish.

Prepare a fire for direct-heat cooking in a grill (see page 10). Position the grill rack 4–6 inches (10–15 cm) above the fire.

Remove the meat from the marinade and pat it dry with paper towels; reserve the marinade.

Arrange the onion slices and bell pepper rings on the rack. Brush them with the olive oil or vegetable oil and sprinkle with salt to taste. Grill for 3 minutes, then turn and again brush with oil. Grill until lightly browned, about 3 minutes longer. Transfer to a platter, separating the onion slices into rings; set aside while you cook the meat.

Place the steak on the rack. Grill, turning and brushing with the reserved marinade every 2 minutes, until done to your liking, about 8 minutes total for rare or 10 minutes for medium.

To serve, cut the steak into thin slices on the diagonal and across the grain. Mound the steak slices on the platter with the onions and peppers. At the table, place the sliced steak on warm tortillas. Top with salsa, guacamole and/or sour cream if desired, then roll up or fold and eat out of hand.

Serves 6

Simple Spareribs

2 slabs pork spareribs, about 6 lb (3 kg) total
2 tablespoons vegetable oil
coarse or kosher salt
freshly ground coarse black pepper

This preparation was inspired by the late James Beard, who liked ribs seasoned with just salt and pepper and roasted at a high temperature. Grilled corn on the cob makes a nice accompaniment.

Prepare a fire for indirect-heat cooking in a covered grill (see page 10). Position the grill rack 4–6 inches (10–15 cm) above the fire.

Pat the ribs dry with paper towels. Rub them with the vegetable oil, then sprinkle liberally on both sides with salt and pepper.

Place the ribs on the center of the rack, cover the grill and open the vents halfway. Cook for 30 minutes, then turn the ribs and cook until well browned on the outside and no longer pink when cut at the bone, 30–40 minutes longer.

To serve, cut the slabs into single-rib pieces and mound on a warmed platter.

Serves 4–6

Wine-Scented Leg of Lamb

⅔ cup (5 fl oz/160 ml) dry red or
white wine

¼ cup (2 fl oz/60 ml) olive oil

3 tablespoons soy sauce

2 tablespoons chopped fresh thyme or
rosemary, or 2 teaspoons dried thyme
or rosemary

2 teaspoons finely grated lemon zest

2 cloves garlic, minced

½ teaspoon salt

½ teaspoon freshly ground pepper

1 leg of lamb, 6–7 lb (3–3.5 kg),
trimmed of visible fat, boned and
butterflied (about 4 lb/2 kg after
trimming and boning) (see note)

*A butterflied leg of lamb is one that is boned and spread out
flat; as a result it cooks more evenly and is easier to carve than
a bone-in leg. Ask your butcher to prepare it for you. This is a
natural with grill-roasted garlic (recipe on page 83) and pilaf
or mashed potatoes.*

*I*n a bowl, whisk together the wine, olive oil, soy sauce,
thyme or rosemary, lemon zest, garlic, salt and pepper.

Place the lamb in a large lock-top plastic bag and pour
in the wine mixture. Press out the air and seal the bag
tightly. Massage the bag gently to distribute the marinade
evenly. Place in a large bowl and refrigerate, turning and
massaging the bag occasionally, for at least 3 hours, or all
day if you wish.

Prepare a fire for direct-heat cooking in a grill (see page 10).
Position the grill rack 4–6 inches (10–15 cm) above the fire.

Remove the lamb from the marinade and pat it dry with
paper towels; reserve the marinade.

Place the lamb on the rack and grill, turning several
times and brushing with the reserved marinade, until done
to your liking when cut into with a knife, or until an
instant-read thermometer inserted into the thickest part of
the leg registers 130°F (54°C) for rare and 140°F (60°C)
for medium, 35–45 minutes.

Remove the lamb from the grill and transfer to a cutting
board. Cover loosely with aluminum foil and let rest for
5 minutes. To serve, carve into thin slices and arrange on
a warmed platter or individual plates.

Serves 6–8

Hamburgers with Grilled Tomatoes

⅔ cup (5 fl oz/160 ml) mayonnaise
1 tablespoon prepared horseradish
2 lb (1 kg) lean ground (minced) beef
2 tablespoons Dijon-style mustard
2 tablespoons Worcestershire sauce
1 teaspoon salt, plus salt to taste
½ teaspoon freshly ground pepper
3 firm but ripe tomatoes, cut into slices
   ½–¾ inch (12 mm–2 cm) thick
3–4 tablespoons olive oil

To ensure the juiciest burgers, handle the meat as little as possible when shaping the patties. For cheeseburgers, place a slice of Swiss or Cheddar cheese on each patty about 1 minute before removing it from the grill. If you like, serve on toasted sourdough, onion or Kaiser rolls.

Prepare a fire for direct-heat cooking in a grill (see page 10). Position the rack 4–6 inches (10–15 cm) above the fire.

In a small bowl, stir together the mayonnaise and horseradish. Cover and refrigerate until serving.

In a large bowl, combine the beef, mustard, Worcestershire sauce, the 1 teaspoon salt and the pepper. Using a fork, stir to combine the ingredients. Divide the meat into 6 equal portions and gently pat and press each portion into a patty about 3 inches (7.5 cm) in diameter and 1 inch (2.5 cm) thick; don't worry about making them perfectly round.

Place the patties on the rack. Grill, turning every 2 minutes, until done to your liking, about 8 minutes total for rare, 10 minutes for medium or 12 minutes for well done. About 4 minutes before the burgers are done, arrange the tomatoes on the rack, sprinkle them with salt to taste and brush with some of the olive oil. Grill for about 2 minutes, then turn and again brush with olive oil. Grill until the tomatoes are very lightly browned on both sides, about 2 minutes longer.

To serve, transfer the burgers to a warmed platter and place the tomato slices atop and around them. Pass the horseradish mayonnaise at the table.

Serves 6

Sesame Flank Steak

¼ cup (2 fl oz/60 ml) vegetable oil

¼ cup (2 fl oz/60 ml) Asian sesame oil

¼ cup (2 fl oz/60 ml) soy sauce

2 tablespoons fresh lemon juice

2 tablespoons peeled and grated
fresh ginger

1 flank steak, about 1½ lb (750 g)

Because flank steaks are thin, the flavor of the sesame marinade will permeate them thoroughly, producing a wonderfully aromatic result. This steak cooks quickly and is easy to do on a small grill or hibachi. Grilled baby bok choy and yellow bell peppers (capsicums) are good accompaniments.

To make the marinade, in a small bowl, whisk together the vegetable oil, sesame oil, soy sauce, lemon juice and ginger. Place the steak in a shallow nonaluminum dish large enough for it to lie flat. Pour the marinade over the steak and turn to coat evenly. Cover and refrigerate, turning the meat occasionally, for at least 3 hours, or all day if you wish.

Prepare a fire for direct-heat cooking in a grill (see page 10). Position the grill rack 4–6 inches (10–15 cm) above the fire.

Remove the steak from the marinade and pat it dry with paper towels; reserve the marinade.

Place the steak on the rack. Grill, turning two or three times and brushing with the reserved marinade, until done to your liking, about 10 minutes total for rare, 12–14 minutes for medium.

Remove the steak from the grill and transfer to a cutting board. Let rest for about 3 minutes. To serve, cut into thin slices on the diagonal and across the grain. Arrange the slices on a warmed platter and serve at once.

Serves 4

Steak Sandwiches with Chive Butter

FOR THE CHIVE BUTTER:

¼ cup (2 oz/60 g) unsalted butter,
   at room temperature
2 tablespoons chopped fresh chives
   or 2 teaspoons dried chives
2 teaspoons fresh lemon juice
½ teaspoon salt
¼ teaspoon freshly ground pepper

FOR THE STEAKS:

4 beef tenderloin fillet steaks, about
   6 oz (185 g) each
salt and freshly ground pepper
4 slices firm-textured white sandwich
   bread
1–1½ cups (1–1½ oz/30–45 g) watercress
   sprigs, large stems removed

These delectable open-faced sandwiches are topped with a pat of chive butter that melts slowly over the steak, forming an instant herb sauce.

To prepare the chive butter, in a small bowl, combine the butter, chives, lemon juice, salt and pepper. Using a fork or wooden spoon, beat vigorously until blended. Transfer to a sheet of plastic wrap and shape into a log about 2 inches (5 cm) long and 1 inch (2.5 cm) in diameter. Wrap in the plastic wrap and chill until firm, about 1 hour, or for up to 3 days.

Prepare a fire for direct-heat cooking in a grill (see page 10). Position the grill rack 4–6 inches (10–15 cm) above the fire.

To prepare the steaks, sprinkle them lightly with salt and pepper and place them on the rack. Grill, turning every 2 minutes, until done to your liking, about 8 minutes total for rare or 10 minutes for medium. About 4 minutes before the steaks are done, arrange the bread slices on the rack and grill, turning once, until lightly browned, about 2 minutes on each side.

To serve, transfer the bread to individual plates. Place a small handful of watercress on each slice of bread and place a steak on the watercress. Cut the chive butter into 4 equal slices and place a slice on each steak. Serve at once.

Serves 4

Hickory-Smoked Fresh Ham

2 tablespoons coarse or kosher salt

2 teaspoons freshly ground pepper

2 teaspoons dried thyme

2 teaspoons dried sage

3 cloves garlic, minced

½ teaspoon ground allspice or cloves

1 shank-end partial leg of pork, about 10½ lb (5.25 kg), trimmed of excess fat and tied for roasting *(see note)*

2 tablespoons vegetable oil or olive oil

A fresh ham is often called leg of pork, and it is large enough to feed a crowd. Have your butcher trim the ham of excess fat and tie it for roasting. Serve with scalloped or mashed potatoes and corn bread.

Soak 3 handfuls (about 5 oz/155 g) of hickory chips in water to cover for about 1 hour.

Prepare a fire for indirect-heat cooking in a covered grill (see page 10). Position the grill rack 4–6 inches (10–15 cm) above the fire.

In a small bowl, stir together the salt, pepper, thyme, sage, garlic and allspice or cloves. Pat the meat dry with paper towels. Rub the entire surface of the meat with the oil, then rub the meat with the salt mixture.

Scoop half of the soaked wood chips out of the water and drop them onto the fire. Place the pork on the center of the rack, cover the grill and open the vents halfway. Cook for about 1 hour. Turn over the roast and add a few more coals to the fire if necessary to maintain a constant temperature. Scoop the remaining wood chips from the water and drop them onto the fire. Continue to cook until the pork is well browned all over and the herb rub has formed a dry, crispy crust, or until an instant-read thermometer inserted into the thickest part of the pork away from the bone registers 160°F (71°C), about 2 hours longer; add a few more coals to the fire as necessary to maintain a constant temperature.

Remove from the grill and transfer to a cutting board. Cover loosely with aluminum foil and let rest for 15 minutes. To serve, snip the strings, carve the meat across the grain into slices about ¼ inch (6 mm) thick and arrange on a warmed platter.

Serves 10–14

Kansas City Beef Brisket

2 teaspoons paprika

1½ teaspoons salt

½ teaspoon freshly ground black pepper

½ teaspoon cayenne pepper

1 beef brisket, 4–5 lb (2–2.5 kg), trimmed of excess fat

2 tablespoons vegetable oil

double recipe midwestern barbecue sauce (*recipe on page 11*)

Brisket of beef, a flavorful but none-too-tender cut, is a perfect choice for slow roasting on a covered grill. Here it's prepared as it is in the BBQ restaurants of Kansas City, Missouri—with plenty of spices and barbecue sauce. Accompany with baked beans.

Soak 3 handfuls (about 5 oz/155 g) of hickory chips in water to cover for about 1 hour.

Prepare a fire for indirect-heat cooking in a covered grill (see page 10). Position the grill rack 4–6 inches (10–15 cm) above the fire.

In a small cup or bowl, stir together the paprika, salt, black pepper and cayenne pepper. Pat the brisket dry with paper towels. Rub the entire surface of the brisket with the vegetable oil, then rub the paprika mixture over the meat.

Scoop half of the soaked wood chips out of the water and drop them onto the fire. Place the brisket on the center of the rack, cover the grill and open the vents slightly less than halfway, or enough to maintain a slow, steady heat. Cook for 1 hour. Turn the brisket, scoop the remaining wood chips from the water and drop them onto the fire. Cook for 1 hour longer. Brush lightly with the sauce, then turn the brisket and cook, turning two or three times and brushing lightly with the sauce, until the brisket is well browned and has formed a crust on the outside, about 3½ hours total. Add more coals to the fire every hour or so as necessary to maintain a constant temperature.

Remove from the grill and let rest for 10 minutes. To serve, carve into thin slices across the grain; the slices will likely crumble a little. Alternatively, pull the meat apart with 2 forks. Arrange the meat on a warmed platter and spoon some of the sauce over the top. Pass the remaining sauce at the table.

Serves 8

Bourbon-Marinated Chuck Roast

⅔ cup (5 fl oz/160 ml) bourbon whiskey
⅓ cup (3 fl oz/80 ml) vegetable oil
⅓ cup (3 fl oz/80 ml) cider vinegar
1 tablespoon Dijon-style mustard
1 teaspoon salt
½ teaspoon freshly ground pepper
1 boneless beef chuck roast, 3–3½ lb
   (1.5–1.75 kg)

Marinating the meat in bourbon, garlic and spices for at least 24 hours yields a roast that is flavorful, if a bit nontraditional. Serve with roasted autumn vegetables (recipe on page 87), or with steamed rice or rice pilaf.

*I*n a small bowl, whisk together the whiskey, vegetable oil, vinegar, mustard, salt and pepper. Place the beef in a large lock-top plastic bag and pour in the whiskey mixture. Press out the air and seal the bag tightly. Massage the bag gently to distribute the marinade evenly. Place in a large bowl and refrigerate, turning and massaging the bag occasionally, for at least 1 day, or for up to 3 days if you wish.

Prepare a fire for indirect-heat cooking in a covered grill (see page 10). Position the grill rack 4–6 inches (10–15 cm) above the fire.

Remove the meat from the marinade and pat it dry with paper towels; reserve the marinade.

Place the meat on the center of the rack, cover the grill and open the vents halfway. Cook, turning three or four times and brushing with the reserved marinade, until the roast is well browned and an instant-read thermometer inserted into the thickest part registers 130°F (54°C) for rare or 140°F (60°C) for medium, 45–60 minutes.

Remove from the grill and transfer to a cutting board. Cover loosely with aluminum foil and let rest for 10 minutes. To serve, carve into thin slices across the grain and arrange on a warmed platter or individual plates.

Serves 6–8

Mustard-Glazed Sausages with Sauerkraut Relish

FOR THE SAUERKRAUT RELISH:

3 cups (1–1¼ lb/500–625 g) sauerkraut
(fresh or canned)

¼ cup (⅓ oz/10 g) chopped fresh parsley

¼ cup (2 fl oz/60 ml) cider vinegar

3 tablespoons olive oil

4 teaspoons sugar

¼ teaspoon freshly ground pepper

FOR THE SAUSAGES:

½ cup (4 oz/125 g) Dijon-style mustard

¼ cup (3 oz/90 g) honey

2 tablespoons white wine vinegar or
cider vinegar

2 lb (1 kg) fresh sausages, one kind or a
combination (see note), 1–1¼ inches
(2.5–3 cm) in diameter

For this recipe, use any type of fresh sausage made from pork, beef or lamb, or a combination. Whichever type you choose, it is important that you cook them fully. You can remove some of the fat, and reduce the tendency toward flare-ups on the fire, by first pricking the sausages several times with a fork, then blanching them in simmering water for about 5 minutes before grilling.

*T*o make the relish, place the sauerkraut in a colander and rinse under cold running water. Drain well, then squeeze with your hands to remove the excess water. In a large bowl, combine the sauerkraut, parsley, vinegar, olive oil, sugar and pepper. Stir and toss with a fork to mix. Cover and refrigerate for at least 2 hours, or up to 3 days, to blend the flavors.

Prepare a fire for direct-heat cooking in a grill (see page 10). Position the grill rack 4–6 inches (10–15 cm) above the fire.

To prepare the sausages, in a small bowl, whisk together the mustard, honey and vinegar; set aside.

Arrange the sausages on the rack. Have a spray bottle of water handy to extinguish flare-ups. Grill, turning frequently, until well browned and fully cooked, 15–18 minutes. During the last 6–8 minutes of grilling, brush the sausages two or three times with the mustard mixture.

To serve, spread the sauerkraut relish on a warmed platter or individual plates and arrange the sausages on top.

Serves 4–6

Pork Loin with Madeira Marinade

1½ cups (12 fl oz/375 ml) Madeira wine

¼ cup (2 fl oz/60 ml) vegetable oil or olive oil

¼ cup (2 fl oz/60 ml) red or white wine vinegar

1 teaspoon salt

1 teaspoon ground allspice

½ teaspoon ground cloves

½ teaspoon freshly ground pepper

1 boneless pork loin, 3½–4 lb (1.75–2 kg), trimmed of excess fat and tied for roasting

This flavorful loin is good with applesauce, or with apple or pear halves prepared as directed in the mixed fruit grill (recipe on page 102) but without the sweet sauce.

*I*n a small bowl, whisk together the wine, oil, vinegar, salt, allspice, cloves and pepper. Place the pork in a large lock-top plastic bag and pour in the wine mixture. Press out the air and seal the bag tightly. Massage the bag gently to distribute the marinade evenly. Place in a large bowl and refrigerate, turning and massaging the bag occasionally, for at least 6 hours, or for up to 2 days if you wish.

Prepare a fire for indirect-heat cooking in a covered grill (see page 10). Position the grill rack 4–6 inches (10–15 cm) above the fire.

Remove the pork from the marinade and pat it dry with paper towels.

Place the pork loin on the center of the rack, cover the grill and open the vents halfway. Cook for 45 minutes, then turn the roast. Add more coals to the fire if necessary to maintain a constant temperature; continue to cook, turning once more, until the meat is no longer pink when cut into at the thickest part, or until an instant-read thermometer inserted into the thickest part of the meat registers 160°F (71°C), 50–60 minutes longer.

Remove from the grill, cover loosely with aluminum foil and let rest for 10 minutes. To serve, snip the strings, carve the meat across the grain into slices ¼ inch (6 mm) thick and arrange on a warmed platter.

Serves 8

Grill-Roasted Garlic

4 heads garlic
2 tablespoons olive oil
1 tablespoon chopped fresh thyme
  or ½ teaspoon dried thyme
½ teaspoon salt
¼ teaspoon freshly ground pepper

Slow cooking turns a head of garlic mellow, with each clove becoming soft and creamy. This makes a delicious accompaniment to wine-scented leg of lamb (recipe on page 65). To eat, squeeze the whole cloves free of their skins and onto crackers or thinly sliced French bread.

Prepare a fire for indirect-heat cooking in a covered grill (see page 10). Position the grill rack 4–6 inches (10–15 cm) above the fire.

Using a sharp knife, slice off the top ¼–½ inch (6–12 mm) from each garlic head. Rub off some of the loose papery skin covering each head, taking care to keep the heads intact. In a small bowl, combine the garlic heads, olive oil, thyme, salt and pepper. Toss to combine and coat the garlic evenly.

Place the garlic heads on the center of the rack, cover the grill and open the vents halfway. Cook, turning the garlic heads three or four times, until the cloves feel very soft when squeezed gently with tongs or your fingers, 35–40 minutes. Don't worry if the skin chars in spots.

Remove from the grill and serve warm (see note).

Serves 4

Ratatouille from the Grill

1 large eggplant (aubergine)

salt for sprinkling, plus 1 teaspoon salt

1 large yellow onion

2 zucchini (courgettes) or yellow crookneck squashes

2 red or green bell peppers (capsicums)

8–10 large fresh mushrooms

¾ cup (6 fl oz/180 ml) olive oil

1 large tomato, peeled, seeded and chopped (*see glossary, page 107*)

3 tablespoons white wine vinegar

2 cloves garlic, minced

½ teaspoon freshly ground pepper

½ cup (¾ oz/20 g) chopped fresh basil or parsley

Here, grilled vegetables are combined to make a backyard version of Provence's famed ratatouille. Because they are grilled, each retains its own character and the ratatouille develops a smoky flavor.

Cover a baking sheet with paper towels. Trim the eggplant and then cut crosswise into slices about ½ inch (12 mm) thick. Sprinkle both sides of each slice lightly with salt. Spread the slices out on the towel-lined baking sheet and cover with more paper towels. Let stand for about 1 hour.

Prepare a fire for direct-heat cooking in a grill (see page 10). Position the grill rack 4–6 inches (10–15 cm) above the fire.

Rinse the eggplant slices and pat them dry with paper towels. Set aside. Prepare the remaining vegetables as follows, setting each aside on a large platter as it is prepared: Cut the onion crosswise into slices ½ inch (12 mm) thick. Halve the squashes lengthwise. Cut the bell peppers crosswise into rings 1 inch (2.5 cm) thick, removing the seeds and ribs from each ring. Trim the stems of the mushrooms but leave them whole.

Arrange the vegetables on the rack and grill, turning two or three times and brushing them with ½ cup (4 fl oz/120 ml) of the olive oil, until lightly browned and tender-crisp when pierced with the tip of a sharp knife, 10–12 minutes. Remove from the grill and let cool. Cut into bite-size pieces.

Meanwhile, in a large serving bowl, stir or whisk together the remaining ¼ cup (2 fl oz/60 ml) olive oil, the tomato, vinegar, garlic, 1 teaspoon salt, the ground pepper and basil or parsley. Add the vegetables and toss gently to combine. Serve at room temperature.

Serves 6

Roasted Autumn Vegetables

2 baking potatoes, about ½ lb (250 g) each

2 sweet potatoes, about ¾ lb (375 g) each

1 acorn squash, about 1½ lb (750 g)

2–3 tablespoons vegetable oil

1 teaspoon salt

½ teaspoon freshly ground pepper

¼ cup (2 oz/60 g) unsalted butter, melted

1 tablespoon chopped fresh sage or thyme, or 1 teaspoon dried sage or thyme, plus fresh sage or thyme sprigs for garnish, optional

Offer this mélange of golden brown, crisp-crusted vegetables as an accompaniment to meat or poultry.

Prepare a fire for indirect-heat cooking in a covered grill (see page 10). Position the grill rack 4–6 inches (10–15 cm) above the fire.

Using a vegetable peeler or a small, sharp knife, peel the baking potatoes, sweet potatoes and acorn squash. Cut them all crosswise into slices about 1 inch (2.5 cm) thick. For the acorn squash, scrape out any seeds and fibers from the center of the slices and discard. In a large bowl, toss the prepared vegetables together with the vegetable oil, salt and pepper. Set aside.

In a small bowl, stir together the melted butter and sage or thyme. Set aside.

Place the vegetables on the center of the rack, cover the grill and open the vents halfway. Cook for 15 minutes, then turn the slices. Cook for 15 minutes longer, then turn again and brush them with the butter mixture. Continue cooking until the vegetables are well browned and tender when pierced with the tip of a sharp knife, 10–15 minutes longer.

To serve, transfer to a platter. Garnish with the sage or thyme sprigs, if using, and serve hot, warm or at room temperature.

Serves 4

Bruschetta Primavera

2 large tomatoes, peeled, seeded and
   diced (see glossary, page 107)
¼ cup (⅓ oz/10 g) chopped fresh parsley
2 tablespoons chopped fresh basil or
   1 teaspoon dried basil
1 large clove garlic, minced, plus
   4–6 garlic cloves, halved
½ teaspoon salt
¼ teaspoon freshly ground pepper
12 slices crusty bread, each about
   ½ inch (12 mm) thick (see note)
⅓–½ cup (3–4 fl oz/80–125 ml) olive oil

*Use a long, slender baguette-type loaf for the bread and cut
the slices on the diagonal. The brief grilling this recipe requires
can easily be done at the last minute over an existing fire.*

Prepare a fire for direct-heat cooking in a grill (see page 10).
Position the grill rack 4–6 inches (10–15 cm) above the fire.

In a small bowl, stir together the tomatoes, parsley, basil,
minced garlic, salt and pepper. Set aside.

Arrange the bread slices on the rack. Grill, turning two or
three times, until the bread is golden brown on both sides,
about 3 minutes total.

Remove from the grill and immediately rub one side of
each slice with a cut garlic clove, pressing the garlic into
the surface of the bread. Brush or drizzle the olive oil
over the same side of the bread. Top each slice with about
2 tablespoons of the tomato mixture and place on a platter.
Serve as soon as possible. If left to stand, the bread will
gradually soften, although it will still taste good.

Serves 4–6

Grilled Fennel and Endive with Olive Vinaigrette

FOR THE OLIVE VINAIGRETTE:

½ cup (2½ oz/75 g) oil-cured black
  olives, pitted

½ cup (4 fl oz/125 ml) olive oil

1 clove garlic, minced

¼ teaspoon salt

¼ teaspoon freshly ground pepper

2 tablespoons white or red wine vinegar

FOR THE VEGETABLES:

3 large fennel bulbs

6 heads Belgian endive (chicory/witloof)

¼ cup (2 fl oz/60 ml) olive oil

½ teaspoon salt

¼ teaspoon freshly ground pepper

The olive vinaigrette is a good match for the strongly flavored vegetables used here. You can also serve them plain, drizzled with just a little lemon juice. Garnish with the feathery tops of the fennel bulbs, if you like.

Prepare a fire for indirect-heat cooking in a covered grill (see page 10). Position the grill rack 4–6 inches (10–15 cm) above the fire.

To prepare the vinaigrette, place the olives in a sieve and rinse briefly with cold water. Drain and pat dry with paper towels. Chop the olives finely and combine them in a small bowl with the olive oil, garlic, salt and pepper. Whisk briskly until smooth and blended, then whisk in the vinegar. Cover and set aside.

To prepare the vegetables, trim off the stems and feathery tops and any bruised outer stalks from the fennel bulbs. Cut each fennel bulb and each endive in half lengthwise. In a large bowl, gently toss the fennel and the endive with the olive oil, salt and pepper.

Place the fennel on the center of the rack, cover the grill and open the vents halfway. Cook for 15 minutes, then turn the fennel and place the endives on the rack. Re-cover and continue to cook, turning the vegetables again after 10 minutes, until they are lightly browned and tender when pierced, 10–15 minutes longer.

Transfer the vegetables to a platter and spoon some of the vinaigrette over them. Serve hot, warm or at room temperature. Pass the remaining vinaigrette at the table.

Serves 6

Stuffed Mushrooms and Summer Squashes

12 large fresh white mushrooms
4 zucchini (courgettes) or yellow
   crookneck squashes
4 tablespoons (2 fl oz/60 ml) olive oil
1 small yellow onion, chopped
1 clove garlic, minced
¾ cup (3 oz/90 g) soda cracker crumbs
   or fine dried bread crumbs
½ cup (2 oz/60 g) freshly grated
   Cheddar or Parmesan cheese
1 tablespoon chopped fresh oregano or
   1 teaspoon dried oregano
½ teaspoon salt, plus salt to taste
¼ teaspoon freshly ground pepper
3 tablespoons heavy (double) cream

These stuffed vegetables are a fine main course for a vegetarian meal, or a choice accompaniment to grilled fish.

Cut or gently pull the stem from each mushroom, forming a hollow in the base of the cap to hold the stuffing; reserve the stems. Halve the squashes lengthwise and, using a teaspoon, scoop out the centers, leaving a shell about ⅓ inch (8 mm) thick; reserve the centers. Set the prepared vegetables aside.

Prepare a fire for indirect-heat cooking in a covered grill (see page 10). Position the grill rack 4–6 inches (10–15 cm) above the fire.

Chop together the squash centers and mushroom stems. In a frying pan over medium-high heat, warm 2 tablespoons of the olive oil. When hot, add the chopped mixture, onion and garlic and cook, stirring occasionally, until tender and any liquid released during cooking has evaporated, about 7 minutes. Scrape into a large bowl and add the crumbs, cheese, oregano, the ½ teaspoon salt, the pepper and cream. Stir and toss with a fork to combine.

Brush the outsides of the squash shells and mushroom caps with the remaining 2 tablespoons oil; sprinkle with salt. Spoon about 2 teaspoons stuffing into each mushroom cap and 2 tablespoons into each squash shell, mounding slightly.

Place the stuffed vegetables on the center of the rack, cover the grill and open the vents halfway. Cook until the stuffing is browned on top and the vegetables are tender when pierced with the tip of a sharp knife, about 20 minutes.

Transfer to a platter. Serve hot or at room temperature.

Serves 3 as a main course or 4–6 as an accompaniment

Parmesan Pita Toasts

4 pita breads, each about 6 inches
  (15 cm) in diameter
½ cup (2 oz/60 g) freshly grated
  Parmesan cheese
olive oil for brushing
salt

Quick to grill over the still-glowing coals of an existing fire, these easy-to-assemble toasts can be placed on the rack after you've removed the main course. Two flour tortillas, stacked one on top of the other with the cheese in between, can be substituted for each pita bread.

Prepare a fire for direct-heat cooking in a grill (see page 10). Position the grill rack 4–6 inches (10–15 cm) above the fire.

Cut the pita breads in half and gently open the pita "pockets." Sprinkle 1 tablespoon of the cheese inside each pocket, then press down firmly on the bread with your hand. Brush both sides of each pita half with the olive oil and sprinkle lightly with salt.

Arrange the pita halves on the rack. Grill, turning two or three times, until the bread is lightly browned and the cheese has melted slightly, 4–5 minutes total.

To serve, cut each half into wedges and arrange on a serving dish. Serve hot.

Serves 4–6

Slow-Cooked Onions with Tarragon Mustard Sauce

FOR THE TARRAGON MUSTARD SAUCE:

2 tablespoons white wine vinegar or
    tarragon vinegar
2 tablespoons Dijon-style mustard
⅓ cup (3 fl oz/80 ml) olive oil
2 tablespoons chopped fresh tarragon
    or 1 teaspoon dried tarragon
¼ teaspoon salt
pinch of freshly ground pepper

FOR THE ONIONS:

4 yellow onions
3 tablespoons olive oil
½ teaspoon salt
¼ teaspoon freshly ground pepper

Roasting vegetables over coals heightens their natural flavors. Whole onions become especially sweet when prepared on a grill. Try serving these with grilled meat or poultry.

Prepare a fire for indirect-heat cooking in a covered grill (see page 10). Position the grill rack 4–6 inches (10–15 cm) above the fire.

To prepare the tarragon mustard sauce, in a small bowl, whisk together the vinegar and mustard. Slowly add the olive oil, whisking constantly to form a smooth, creamy sauce. Whisk in the tarragon, salt and pepper. Cover and set aside.

To prepare the onions, peel them carefully; take care to keep their layers intact at the root ends, which will help hold them together during cooking. Using a sharp knife and starting at the stem end, slice an X in each onion to within about 1 inch (2.5 cm) of the root end. In a large bowl, toss the onions with the olive oil, salt and pepper.

Place the onions on the center of the rack, cover the grill and open the vents halfway. Cook, turning the onions every 15–20 minutes, until they are tender when pierced with the tip of a sharp knife, 45–50 minutes total.

To serve, transfer the onions to a platter and drizzle some of the sauce over them. Serve hot, warm or at room temperature. Pass the remaining sauce at the table.

Serves 4

Stuffed Acorn Squash

¼ cup (2 oz/60 g) unsalted butter

½ cup (2½ oz/75 g) finely chopped onion

½ cup (2½ oz/75 g) finely chopped celery

2 cups (4 oz/125 g) fresh white bread crumbs

1 teaspoon dried sage

½ teaspoon salt, plus salt to taste

¼ teaspoon freshly ground pepper, plus pepper to taste

½ cup (3 oz/90 g) chopped prunes

¼ cup (1 oz/30 g) chopped walnuts

3 tablespoons water

2 acorn squashes

This savory stuffing is infused with the sweetness of prunes. For a heartier dish, add some cooked ground (minced) beef or sausage to the mixture.

Prepare a fire for indirect-heat cooking in a covered grill (see page 10). Position the grill rack 4–6 inches (10–15 cm) above the fire.

In a frying pan over medium heat, melt the butter. When hot, add the onion and celery and cook, stirring frequently, until softened and wilted slightly, about 5 minutes. Scrape into a large bowl and add the bread crumbs, sage, ½ teaspoon salt, ¼ teaspoon pepper, prunes and walnuts. Sprinkle the water over the top. Stir and toss with a fork to distribute the ingredients evenly. Set aside.

Cut out four 6-inch (15-cm) squares of aluminum foil; set aside. Using a large, sharp knife, cut each squash in half through the stem end. Using a spoon, scrape out the seeds and any fibers and discard. Season the cut sides generously with salt and pepper. Divide the bread crumb mixture evenly among the squash cavities, pressing it down lightly. To prevent the stuffing from drying out, cover each squash with a square of foil, folding it down over the sides.

Place the stuffed squashes, foil side up, on the center of the rack, cover the grill and open the vents halfway. Cook for 45 minutes. Remove the foil and continue cooking in the covered grill until the squash is tender when pierced and the stuffing is lightly browned, about 15 minutes longer.

Transfer to a warmed platter and serve at once.

Serves 4

Grilled Bananas and Pineapple with Butterscotch Sauce

For the butterscotch sauce:

½ cup (4 oz/125 g) unsalted butter

1 cup (7 oz/220 g) firmly packed brown
  sugar

½ cup (4 fl oz/125 ml) heavy (double)
  cream

pinch of salt

½ teaspoon vanilla extract (essence)

For the fruit:

4 firm but ripe bananas

6–8 fresh pineapple spears, ½–1 inch
  (12 mm–2.5 cm) thick, or canned
  pineapple spears, drained

6 tablespoons (3 oz/90 g) unsalted butter

2 tablespoons granulated sugar

¼ teaspoon ground nutmeg

This unusual dessert is attractive garnished with strips of orange zest. For a splurge, serve the warm grilled fruit over vanilla ice cream.

Prepare a fire for direct-heat cooking in a grill (see page 10). Position the grill rack 4–6 inches (10–15 cm) above the fire.

To prepare the butterscotch sauce, in a small saucepan over medium heat, melt the butter. Add the brown sugar and cream and bring to a boil, whisking almost constantly. Remove from the heat and stir in the salt and vanilla. Cover to keep warm. (If made ahead, let cool, then cover and refrigerate for up to 1 week. Reheat over low heat before serving.)

To prepare the fruit, peel the bananas. Place the bananas and the pineapple spears on a platter and set aside. In a small saucepan over medium heat, combine the butter, granulated sugar and nutmeg, and stir frequently until melted and smooth. Remove from the heat and pour over the fruit. Turn the fruit to coat evenly with the butter mixture.

Arrange the pineapple spears and the bananas on the rack and grill, turning every 2–3 minutes, until the fruit is lightly browned and the bananas are just tender when pierced with the tip of a sharp knife, 10–12 minutes total.

Remove from the grill and arrange on a warmed platter. Reheat the sauce to serving temperature, if necessary. Spoon some of the warm butterscotch sauce over the fruit. Pass the remaining sauce at the table.

Serves 6–8

Mixed Fruit Grill with Spiced Lemon Cream

For the spiced lemon cream:

¾ cup (6 fl oz/180 ml) heavy (double) cream, chilled

1 tablespoon nonfat dry milk

¼ cup (3 oz/90 g) honey

2 teaspoons finely grated lemon zest

1 tablespoon fresh lemon juice

¼ teaspoon ground cinnamon

For the fruit:

4 apples, preferably Golden Delicious

4 firm but ripe pears, preferably Bosc

3 tablespoons unsalted butter, melted

2 tablespoons sugar

Apples and pears are delicious grilled, but you can substitute them with any of your own fresh, seasonal favorites. Note that apples and pears take about twice as long to cook as summer fruits such as apricots and peaches. To prepare most fruits, halve them, then pit or core. If the skin is tough, peel before cooking; for summer fruits, peeling usually isn't necessary.

Prepare a fire for direct-heat cooking in a grill (see page 10). Position the grill rack 4–6 inches (10–15 cm) above the fire.

To prepare the spiced lemon cream, in a small bowl, combine the cream and the dry milk. Using a wire whisk or an electric mixer, beat until stiff peaks form, then fold in the honey, lemon zest, lemon juice and cinnamon. Cover and refrigerate until serving.

To prepare the fruit, halve, peel and core the apples and pears. Place the fruit in a large bowl and toss with the melted butter and sugar.

Arrange the fruit, cut side down, on the rack. Grill, turning every 10 minutes, until lightly browned and tender but not mushy when pierced with the tip of a sharp knife, 25–30 minutes total.

To serve, transfer to a platter or individual plates. Serve warm or at room temperature. Pass the lemon cream at the table.

Serves 6–8

Glossary

The following glossary defines terms specifically as they relate to outdoor cooking. Included are major and unusual ingredients and basic techniques.

Asparagus
At their best in April and May, these bright green, purplish green or sometimes pale ivory-green spears should be trimmed before cooking. Look for firm, brightly colored spears with tightly furled tips.

Beets
Root vegetable prized for its naturally sweet flavor. The most common variety is bright purplish red, but gold, white and striped beets are also available. For the best texture and taste, choose beets no larger than about 2 inches (5 cm) in diameter.

Belgian Endive
Leaf vegetable with refreshing, slightly bitter, spear-shaped leaves, white to pale yellow-green—or sometimes red—in color and tightly packed in cylindrical heads 4–6 inches (10–15 cm) long. Also known as chicory or witloof.

Bell Pepper
Sweet-fleshed, bell-shaped member of the pepper family. Also known as capsicum. Most common in the unripe green form, although ripened red or yellow varieties are also available. Creamy pale yellow, orange and purple-black types may also be found.

To prepare a raw bell pepper, cut it in half lengthwise with a sharp knife. Pull out the stem section from each half, along with the cluster of seeds attached to it. Remove any remaining seeds, along with any thin white membranes, or ribs, to which they are attached. Cut the pepper halves into quarters, strips or thin slices, as called for in the specific recipe.

Bourbon
American form of whiskey, used in some barbecue marinades, bastes and sauces. Made from at least 51 percent corn, plus other grains, and aged for at least 2 years in new, charred-oak barrels that impart a smoky, slightly sweet flavor and rich caramel color to the spirit.

Bread Crumbs
Fresh or dried bread crumbs are sometimes used as a coating for foods or to add body and texture to fillings.

To make bread crumbs, choose a good-quality rustic loaf made of unbleached wheat flour, with a firm, coarse-textured crumb. For fresh crumbs, cut away the crusts and crumble the bread by hand into a blender or a food processor fitted with the metal blade and process until fine crumbs form. For dried crumbs, spread the fresh crumbs on a baking pan. Dry slowly in an oven set at its lowest temperature for about 1 hour. Fine dried bread crumbs are also sold prepackaged in food markets.

Chili, Jalapeño
Small, thick-fleshed, fiery chili, usually sold green, although red ripened specimens can sometimes be found.

When handling chilies, wear kitchen gloves to prevent any cuts or abrasions on your hands from contacting the peppers' volatile oils; once finished, wash your hands well with warm, soapy water, and take special care not to touch your eyes or other sensitive areas.

Chili Oil
Popular seasoning made of **sesame** or **vegetable oil** in which hot chilies have been steeped. Available in Asian markets and the specialty-food section of most food stores.

Coconut Milk
Although commonly thought to be the thin, relatively clear liquid found inside a whole coconut, coconut milk is actually an extract made from shredded fresh coconut. Good-quality unsweetened coconut milk is available in cans in some food markets.

Cornstarch
Fine, powdery flour ground from the endosperm of corn—the white heart of the kernel—and, because it contains no gluten, used as a thickening agent in some bastes and sauces. Also known as cornflour.

Cream, Heavy
Whipping cream with a butterfat content of at least 36 percent. For the best flavor and cooking properties, purchase 100 percent natural fresh cream with a short shelf life printed on the carton; avoid long-lasting varieties that have been processed by ultraheat methods. In Britain, use double cream in place of heavy cream.

Eggplant
Vegetable-fruit, also known as aubergine, with tender, mildly earthy, sweet flesh. The shiny skins of eggplants vary in color from purple to red and from yellow to white, and their shapes range from small and oval to long and slender to large and pear shaped. The most common variety is the large, purple globe eggplant, which, because it sometimes tends to have a slightly bitter edge, is usually sliced and lightly salted to draw out its juices before cooking. Slender, purple Asian eggplants are more tender, sweeter and have fewer, smaller seeds.

Fennel
Crisp, mildly anise-flavored bulb vegetable (below), sometimes called by its Italian name, *finocchio*. Another related variety of the bulb is valued for its fine, feathery leaves and stems, which are used as a fresh or dried herb, and for its small, crescent-shaped seeds, which are dried and used as a spice.

Garlic
Pungent bulb popular worldwide as a flavoring ingredient, both raw and cooked. For the best flavor, purchase whole heads of dry garlic, separating individual cloves from the head as needed; it is best not to purchase more than you will use in 1 or 2 weeks, as garlic can shrivel and lose its flavor with prolonged storage.

To peel a garlic clove, place on a work surface and cover with the flat side of a large chef's knife.

Press down firmly but carefully on the side of the knife to crush the clove slightly; the dry skin will then slip off easily.

GINGER, FRESH
The rhizome of the tropical ginger plant, which yields a sweet, strong-flavored spice. Whole ginger rhizomes, commonly but mistakenly called roots, can be purchased fresh in food stores or vegetable markets.

Before slicing, chopping or grating fresh ginger, the rhizome's brown, papery skin is usually peeled away. The ginger may then be sliced or chopped with a knife, or grated against the fine holes of a grater.

MADEIRA
Sweet, amber-colored dessert wine originating on the Portuguese island of Madeira. Used in some marinades and sauces.

MUSTARDS
Dijon mustard is made in Dijon, France, from brown mustard seeds (unless marked *blanc*) and white wine or wine vinegar. Pale in color, fairly hot and sharp tasting, true Dijon mustard and non-French blends labeled "Dijon-style" are widely available. Coarse-grained mustards, which have a granular texture due to roughly ground mustard seeds, include the French *moutarde de Meaux* and some high-quality British and German varieties.

OILS
In outdoor cooking, oils—used on their own or as part of marinades, bastes or sauces—not only prevent foods from sticking to the grill, but can also subtly enhance their flavor. Store all oils in airtight containers away from heat and light.

Olive Oil Extra-virgin olive oil, extracted from olives on the first pressing without use of heat or chemicals, is prized for its pure, fruity taste and golden to pale green hue. The higher-priced extra-virgin olive oils are usually of better quality. Products labeled "pure olive oil," less aromatic and flavorful, may be used for all-purpose cooking.

HERBS
Many fresh and dried herbs alike can be used to bring aromatic distinction to outdoor cooking. Some used in this book include:

Basil Sweet, spicy herb (below) popular in Italian and French cooking.

Chives Long, thin green shoot with a mild flavor reminiscent of the onion, to which it is related. Although chives are available dried in the herb-and-spice section of food stores, fresh chives possess the best flavor.

Cilantro Green, leafy herb (below) resembling flat-leaf (Italian) **parsley**, with a sharp, aromatic, somewhat astringent flavor. Popular in Latin American and Asian cuisines. Also called fresh coriander and Chinese parsley.

Dill Fine, feathery leaves with a sweet, aromatic flavor. Used fresh or dried.

Mint Refreshing herb available in many varieties, with spearmint the most common. Used fresh or dried to flavor a broad range of dishes.

Oregano Aromatic, pungent and spicy Mediterranean herb (below), also known as wild marjoram. Used fresh or dried as a seasoning for all kinds of savory dishes. Especially popular in dishes featuring tomatoes and other vegetables.

Parsley This popular fresh herb is available in two varieties, the readily available curly-leaf type and a flat-leaf type (below). The latter, also known as Italian parsley, has a more pronounced flavor and is generally preferred.

Rosemary Mediterranean herb (below), used either fresh or dried, with an aromatic flavor well suited to lamb, as well as poultry, seafood and vegetables.

Sage Pungent herb (below), used either fresh or dried, that goes particularly well with fresh or cured pork, lamb and poultry.

Tarragon Fragrant, distinctively sweet herb used fresh or dried as a seasoning for seafood, chicken, light meats and vegetables.

Thyme Fragrant, clean-tasting, small-leaved herb (below) popular fresh or dried as a seasoning for poultry, light meats, seafood and vegetables.

Chopping Fresh Herbs
Wash the herbs under cold running water and thoroughly shake dry. If the herb has leaves attached along woody stems, pull the leaves from the stems, otherwise, hold the stems together. Gather up the leaves into a tight, compact bunch. Using a chef's knife, carefully cut across the bunch to chop the leaves coarsely. Discard the stems. Continue chopping the leaves to the desired fineness.

Peanut Oil Peanut oil has a subtle hint of the peanut's richness.

Sesame Oil Flavorful sesame oil is pressed from sesame seeds. Asian sesame oils, from China and Japan, are made from toasted sesame seeds, resulting in a dark, strong oil used primarily as a flavoring ingredient.

Vegetable Oils Flavorless vegetable and seed oils such as safflower, canola and corn oil are employed for their high cooking temperatures and bland flavor.

ONIONS
Used as a seasoning or as ingredients in their own right, all manner of onions bring pungent-sweet distinction to outdoor cooking. Green onions, also called spring onions or scallions, are a variety harvested immature, leaves and all, before their bulbs have formed. The green and white parts may both be enjoyed for their mild but still pronounced onion flavor. Red (Spanish) onions are a mild, sweet variety with purplish red skin and red-tinged white flesh. Yellow onions are the common, white-fleshed, strong-flavored variety distinguished by their dry, yellowish brown skins.

SALT, COARSE OR KOSHER
Kosher and coarse-grained salts, sold in the seasonings section of food stores, are well suited for use in dry and wet marinades and seasonings. Sea salt is an acceptable substitute.

SAUERKRAUT
Shredded cabbage preserved in a salty brine, which gives it a bracingly tangy flavor and crisp texture. Sold either fresh in delicatessens and specialty markets, or canned in food stores, it is generously rinsed with fresh water and squeezed dry before use to eliminate some of the saltiness.

SHALLOTS
Small member of the onion family with brown skin, white-to-purple flesh and a flavor resembling a cross between sweet onion and **garlic.**

SHERRY, DRY
Fortified, cask-aged wine, ranging in varieties from dry to sweet, enjoyed as an aperitif and sometimes used as a flavoring in marinades.

SHRIMP
Raw shrimp (prawns) are generally sold with the heads already removed but the shells still intact. Before cooking they are usually peeled and their thin, veinlike intestinal tracts removed.

To peel and devein shrimp, use your thumbs to split open the shrimp's thin shell along the concave side, between its two rows of legs. Grasp the shell and gently peel it away.

SPICES
Savory, hot and sweet, the following spices—derived from the aromatic seeds, bark or roots of various plants— all add distinctive flavor to outdoor dishes:

Allspice Sweet spice of Caribbean origin (below) with a flavor suggesting a blend of **cinnamon, cloves** and **nutmeg.**

Cayenne Pepper Very hot ground spice derived from dried cayenne chili peppers.

Celery Seeds Small, dried pale green seeds of the familiar vegetable, sold in the spice section of food stores and used whole as a seasoning to add a subtle celery flavor.

Chili Powder Commercial blend of spices featuring ground dried chili peppers along with such other seasonings as cumin, **oregano, cloves,** coriander, **pepper** and **salt.** Best purchased in small quantities, as flavor diminishes rapidly after opening.

Cinnamon Popular spice derived from the aromatic bark of a type of evergreen tree; sold as whole dried strips (below) or ground.

Cloves Rich and aromatic East African spice used whole or in its

ground form to flavor both savory and sweet recipes.

Curry Powder Generic term for blends of spices commonly used to flavor East Indian–style dishes. Most curry powders will include coriander, cumin, **chili powder,** fenugreek and **turmeric;** other possible additions include cardamom, **cinnamon, cloves, allspice,** fennel seeds and **ginger.** Best purchased in small quantities, as flavor diminishes rapidly after opening.

Mustard Seeds Small, spherical seeds of the mustard plant, used to season brines, marinades and sauces, as well as to make homemade mustards.

Nutmeg The hard pit of the fruit of the nutmeg tree. May be bought already ground or, for fresher flavor, whole to be grated fresh as needed.

Paprika Powdered spice derived from the dried paprika pepper; available in sweet, mild and hot forms.

Peppercorns Pepper, the most common savory spice, is best purchased as whole peppercorns (below), to be ground in a pepper mill as needed, or coarsely crushed. Black peppercorns derive from slightly underripe pepper berries, whose hulls oxidize as they dry.

Red Pepper Flakes Coarse flakes of dried red chilies, including seeds, which add moderately hot flavor to the foods they season.

Turmeric Pungent, earthy ground spice that imparts a vibrant yellow color to any dish.

Using a small knife, make a shallow slit along the peeled shrimp's back, just deep enough to expose the long, veinlike intestinal tract. With the tip of the knife or your fingers, lift up and pull out the vein, discarding it.

SOY SAUCE
Asian seasoning and condiment made from soybeans, wheat, salt and water. Seek out good-quality imported soy sauces; Chinese brands tend to be markedly saltier than Japanese.

SQUASH, ACORN
Variety of hard winter squash with a shape reminiscent of an acorn, with tough green skin and sweet, orange flesh. Other winter squashes such as smaller butternuts or pumpkins may be substituted.

SUGAR
Sugar may be used in marinades and barbecue sauces to add a subtle sweetness to grilled foods and, by caramelizing under intense heat, to give a finished dish a rich, deep brown glaze. Sugar-laden sauces burn easily and should be brushed on food during the last 15–20 minutes of cooking. Granulated sugar is the standard, widely used form of pure white sugar; do not use superfine granulated sugar, also known as castor sugar, unless specified. Brown sugar, commonly available in food stores, is a rich-tasting form of granulated sugar combined with molasses in varying quantities to yield golden, light or dark brown sugar, with crystals varying from coarse to finely granulated.

TOMATOES
During summer, when tomatoes are in season, use the best sun-ripened tomatoes you can find. At other times of year, plum tomatoes, sometimes called Roma or egg tomatoes, are likely to have the best flavor and texture.

To peel fresh tomatoes, bring a saucepan of water to a boil. Using a small, sharp knife, cut out the core from the stem end. Cut a shallow X in the skin at the tomato's base. Submerge for about 20 seconds in the boiling water, then remove and dip in a bowl of cold water. Starting at the X, peel the skin using your fingertips and, if necessary, the knife blade.

Cut the tomatoes in half and turn each half cut-side down. Then cut as directed in individual recipes.

To seed a tomato, cut it in half crosswise. Squeeze to force out the seed sacs.

TEQUILA
The best-known Mexican spirit, a powerful clear or golden liquid distilled from the juice of the blue agave (century) plant. Sometimes used as a flavorful addition to marinades.

TORTILLAS, FLOUR
Thin, flat, round unleavened Mexican bread made from wheat flour; used as an edible wrapper for meat, poultry, seafood, cheese and other foods. Commercially manufactured tortillas are widely available in well-stocked food stores and ethnic markets.

VANILLA EXTRACT
Vanilla beans are dried aromatic pods of a variety of orchid; one of the most popular sweet flavorings. Vanilla is most commonly used in the form of an alcohol-based extract (essence); be sure to purchase products labeled "pure vanilla extract." Vanilla extract from Madagascar is the best.

VERMOUTH, DRY WHITE
Dry wine commercially enhanced with herbs and barks to give it an aromatic flavor.

VINEGARS
Literally "sour wine," vinegar results when certain strains of yeast cause wine or some other alcoholic liquid such as apple cider to ferment for a second time, turning it acidic. The best-quality wine vinegars begin with good quality wine. Red wine vinegar, like the wine from which it is made, has a more robust flavor than vinegar produced from white wine. Cider vinegar has the sweet tang and golden color of the apple cider from which it is made. Flavored vinegars are made by adding herbs such as **tarragon** and **dill** or fruits such as raspberries.

WATERCRESS
Refreshing, slightly peppery, dark green leaf vegetable commercially cultivated and also found wild in freshwater streams. Most often torn by hand into bite-sized sprigs, it is used primarily in salads and as a popular garnish.

WORCESTERSHIRE SAUCE
Traditional English seasoning or condiment; an intensely flavorful, savory and aromatic blend of many ingredients, including molasses, **soy sauce, garlic, onion** and anchovies. Popular as a marinade ingredient or table sauce for grilled foods, especially red meats.

ZEST
Thin, brightly colored, outermost layer of a citrus fruit's peel, containing most of its aromatic essential oils—a lively source of flavor. Zest may be removed with a simple tool known as a zester (below), drawn across the fruit's skin to remove the zest in thin strips.

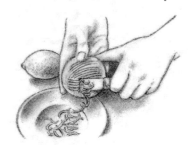

Zest can also be removed with a fine hand-held grater, or in wide strips with a vegetable peeler or a paring knife held almost parallel to the fruit's skin. Zest removed with the latter two tools may then be thinly sliced or chopped on a cutting board.

Index

apple-mint relish, turkey burgers with 42
asparagus and salmon, lemon-dill 26

bacon-wrapped Cornish hens 33
bacon-wrapped scallop and salmon skewers 24
bananas and pineapples, grilled, with butterscotch sauce 101
beef
    beef brisket, Kansas City 75
    chuck roast, bourbon-marinated 77
    flank steak, sesame 68
    hamburgers with grilled tomatoes 66
    rib roast, old-fashioned 57
    short ribs 58
    steak fajitas 61
    steak sandwiches with chive butter 71
    top round with jalapeño marinade 53
beet relish, tuna with 19
bourbon-marinated chuck roast 77
bruschetta primavera 88
burgers
    with grilled tomatoes 66
    lamb and eggplant 54
    turkey, with apple-mint relish 42
butterscotch sauce, grilled bananas and pineapple with 101

chicken
    breasts, tropical 39
    breasts with black olive butter 30
    deviled 41
    grill-roasted, with potato fans 49
    Jamaican jerk 29
    tandoori 45
chive butter, steak sandwiches with 71
Cornish hens, bacon-wrapped 33

deviled chicken 41
direct-heat cooking 10
duck, orange-roasted 35

eggplant
    and lamb burgers 54
    ratatouille from the grill 84
endive and fennel, grilled, with olive vinaigrette 91
equipment 6–9

fajitas, steak 61
fennel and endive, grilled, with olive vinaigrette 91
fire, building a 10
fish
    halibut with grilled pipérade 15
    salmon, lemon-dill, and asparagus 26
    scallop and salmon skewers, bacon-wrapped 24
    swordfish, Thai-style, with lime and cilantro sauce 23
    tuna with beet relish 19
flavor, enhancing 11
fruit. See also individual fruits
    mixed fruit grill with spiced lemon cream 102

garlic, grill-roasted 83
grills and accessories 8–9

halibut with grilled pipérade 15
ham, hickory-smoked fresh 72
hamburgers with grilled tomatoes 66

indirect-heat cooking 10

Jamaican jerk chicken 29

Kansas City beef brisket 75

lamb
    and eggplant burgers 54
    wine-scented leg of 65
lemon-dill salmon and asparagus 26

marinades. See sauces and marinades
midwestern barbecue sauce 11

mop sauce, spicy 12
mushrooms
    and shrimp skewers 20
    and summer squashes, stuffed 92
mustard-glazed sausages with sauerkraut relish 78

olive vinaigrette, grilled fennel and endive with 91
onions, slow-cooked, with tarragon mustard sauce 97
orange-roasted duck 35

Parmesan pita toasts 94
peanut dipping sauce 13
pepper relish, sweet-and-hot, tea-smoked shrimp with 16
pineapples and bananas, grilled, with butterscotch sauce 101
pipérade, grilled, halibut with 15
pita toasts, Parmesan 94
pork
    fresh ham, hickory-smoked 72
    loin with Madeira marinade 80
    spareribs, simple 62
potato fans, grill-roasted chicken with 49

ratatouille from the grill 84
ribs
    beef short 58
    spareribs, simple 62

salmon and asparagus, lemon-dill 26
salmon and scallop skewers, bacon wrapped 24
sauces and marinades
    midwestern barbecue sauce 11
    peanut dipping sauce 13
    red or white wine barbecue sauce 12
    soy-ginger marinade 13
    spicy mop sauce 12
sausages
    mustard-glazed, with sauerkraut relish 78
    turkey, with chutney mustard 50

scallop and salmon skewers, bacon wrapped 24
sesame flank steak 68
shrimp
    and mushroom skewers 20
    tea-smoked, with sweet-and-hot pepper relish 16
skewers
    bacon-wrapped scallop and salmon 24
    shrimp and mushroom 20
    turkey kabobs with peanut dipping sauce 36
soy-ginger marinade 13
spiced lemon cream, mixed fruit grill with 102
squashes
    stuffed acorn 98
    stuffed mushrooms and summer squashes 92
steak fajitas 61
steak sandwiches with chive butter 71
swordfish, Thai-style, with lime and cilantro sauce 23

tandoori chicken 45
tarragon mustard sauce, slow cooked onions with 97
tea-smoked shrimp with sweet-and-hot pepper relish 16
Thai-style swordfish with lime and cilantro sauce 23
tomatoes, grilled, hamburgers with 66
tropical chicken breasts 39
tuna with beet relish 19
turkey
    burgers with apple-mint relish 42
    hickory-smoked thighs 46
    kabobs with peanut dipping sauce 36
    sausages with chutney mustard 50

vegetables. See also individual vegetables
    ratatouille from the grill 84
    roasted autumn 87

ACKNOWLEDGMENTS

The publishers would like to thank the following people for their generous assistance and support in producing this book: Stephen W. Griswold, Sharon C. Lott, Laurie Wertz, Ken DellaPenta, Ruth Jacobson, Katherine Withers-Cobbs, Tina Schmitz, the buyers and store managers for Pottery Barn and Williams-Sonoma stores.

The following kindly lent props for the photography: American Rag-Maison, Biordi Art Imports, Candelier, Fillamento, Forrest Jones, RH Shop, Sue Fisher King, Chuck Williams, Williams-Sonoma and Pottery Barn.